MW00627796

MODERN
COLLEGE

Choose Your Path.

Get a Degree.

Land Your Dream Job.

ALEX VALAITIS

Modern College LLC

Modern College is a work of nonfiction. Some names and identifying details have been changed.

Published by Modern College LLC

Copyright © 2020 by Alex Valaitis
All rights reserved

No part of this publication may be reproduced, distributed, or transmitted in any form or by any means, including photocopying, recording, or other electronic or mechanical methods, without the prior written permission of the publisher, except in the case of brief quotations embodied in reviews and certain other non-commercial uses permitted by copyright law.

Paperback ISBN: 978-1-7352067-0-7
Ebook ISBN: 978-1-7352067-1-4
Hardback ISBN: 978-1-7352067-2-1

Editors: Barbara Schirmer, Jennifer Rees
Cover design: David Provolo
Illustrations: Amanda Valaitis

Get more Modern College content:

Website: TheModernCollege.com
Facebook: Facebook.com/ModernCollegePage
LinkedIn: Linkedin.com/company/the-modern-college

Connect with Alex Valaitis:

Follow Alex on Twitter: @alex_valaitis
Follow Alex on Instagram: AlexValaitis
Follow Alex on LinkedIn: linkedin.com/in/alexvalaitis/

To my Grandpa "Poppy" Joe and Grandma "Cookie" Carolyn.
My 2 guardian angels who always preached
the importance of college.
Thank you both for providing me the greatest gift
of all, an education.

I strive every day to make you both proud.

CONTENTS

Part 1: Choose Your Path

Part 2: Get a Degree

Part 3: Land Your Dream Job

INTRODUCTION

Society has changed a lot over the years, but the advice that we give to college students has not.

Why did I write this book?

To be clear, I tried really hard not to write this book. After I graduated from the University of Wisconsin-Madison in December of 2016, I was excited to start the journey into the workforce that my education had prepared me for, and to leave college in the rearview for good. Within a week of walking across the stage for graduation, I was on a one-way flight to Paris with nothing but a backpack, my iPhone, and time to explore. My solo trip to Europe represented the fruits of my labor in college. Four and a half years of pure grinding had landed me a full-time offer out in Silicon Valley and enough money in the bank to cover my expenses in the months before

I began my first day of work. I used that financial cushion to travel to six different countries and see what the world had to offer. I sipped espressos in Paris, attended all night raves in Berlin, snowboarded in the Swiss Alps, and visited historical sites like the Colosseum in Rome. With each new experience, the pain from long hours spent in the library studying for exams began to fade. My faith in the system had been restored, at least to some degree.

Two months later I returned to the States, packed up my Subaru Tribeca, and convinced my best friend, Ivan, to accompany me on the drive from Wisconsin to San Francisco. As I gave my family members parting hugs and pulled out of my driveway, I couldn't help but reflect on the moment at hand. The past four and a half years hadn't been perfect, but my college experience had set me up excellently for the next phase of my life. I was entering a new job in product management at Intuit with a starting pay in the six figures and awesome benefits. By most measures, I had already achieved key aspects of the American dream and had every reason to be happy. However, there was a part of me that couldn't help but feel a sense of guilt. While I was beginning the next phase of my life on a high note, many of my childhood friends and former classmates from over the years were not.

These acquaintances didn't get awesome trips to Europe or high-paying jobs to look forward to; instead, they were getting mattresses in their parents' basements. It wasn't like all of these people were slackers either; in fact, most of them held degrees from highly reputable universities. Yet, somewhere along the way, the higher education system had failed them. Instead of their college experiences propelling them forward in life, they had in some ways moved backward, with many of them not only lacking employment but also saddled with tens of thousands of dollars in student debt. It didn't seem right, and I couldn't get these friends out of my head as I drove across the country. Had I simply been lucky? What had I done differently in my college years that we had landed in such different places? Deep inside, I knew that I had discovered a formula for success. I just didn't know how to articulate it.

To help calm my mind, I decided to publish my first article on the blogging platform Medium while in a hotel room in Salt Lake City, one of our stops on the way to San Francisco. I titled it *5 Tips to Land Internships & Jobs as a College Student.* To my surprise, the article was a hit and I soon began receiving dozens of messages on LinkedIn and Facebook from current college students thanking me for the advice. I was deeply moved by the responses and felt a sense of fulfillment that I hadn't felt in a long time.

I used the positive response as fuel to move forward and in the following months, I found myself blogging much more often online. I wrote about everything from how to write more frequently, human immortality, traveling through Europe, and my encounter with Uber's controversial founder, Travis Kalanick. However, I found myself gravitating back to college advice once more when I published a post titled, *3 Reasons Why You Should Double Major in College.* It was after this post that I truly recognized the huge demand among college students for relevant advice. Clearly, many students in college were looking for guidance, but why were they resorting to reading advice from someone like me? I felt under-qualified to be providing information to anyone on the internet, let alone trying to guide anyone. After all, I was only 22 years old and just getting my first taste of the real world. Yet, I was intrigued so I began scouring the internet for advice catered to people in college.

I soon began to pick up on a trend. Much of the content surrounding college advice was grossly outdated and no longer relevant. All of the books and articles I had found were written by people who had graduated college many years (if not decades) earlier. The advice they offered was centered around a college experience that was fundamentally different than the modern college environment and society as a whole. Most of the authors had graduated from college before the advent of the internet, a creation that profoundly changed the college experience and continues to shape the educational landscape to this day. Imagine attending college without the existence of Google or the iPhone! Technology is a vital tool for finding success in both college and the professional world today. When used well, it is the ultimate equalizer. But when ignored or used poorly, it can be destructive. To talk about college without a deep understanding of the role of technology is akin to taking a butter knife to a gunfight. Similarly, these authors didn't understand the weight of student debt on the contemporary college experience. College has become too expensive for students to pursue as simply a means of intellectual exploration. To justify the costs, students expect higher education to serve a more tangible purpose and lead to economic opportunity upon graduation.

And that's when it hit me. Was I, in fact, an expert in the modern college experience? Expert felt like too strong of a word, yet I couldn't help but rank my guidance and advice as substantially above much of the content on the internet and published in books by alleged authorities. Only a small percentage of these authors had experienced college as recently as I had and of that subset of people, most had left college behind to focus on the path ahead. On the other hand, I had a vested interest, which was based on guiding my younger brother, Austin, through his college experience. I first contemplated writing a comprehensive college guide for Austin and his friends, but then I realized that I could help a much larger audience of students. With the realization that I was sufficiently knowledgeable and experienced to give advice to the inexperienced, I had no choice but to write this book.

Who am I?

You may be skeptical that I am the right person to be giving advice on college, and that is totally reasonable. While I graduated recently, so did millions of other people. So, let me explain a few things that make me uniquely positioned to offer such advice.

The first is that I was able to find professional success immediately out of college. I don't say this to be boastful or to diminish others but just to explain one reason that I am able to offer advice to those hoping for the same outcome from their college experience. If you want to find success immediately after college, you should seek advice from others who have actually done it. That's what I did while in school, and it worked. The advice in this book is what I followed throughout my own journey in college and into the "real world".

The second is that at the time of this writing, I am fortunate to work for a company that is at the top in the world when it comes to professional networking, job opportunities, and online education. The vision of LinkedIn is to "create economic opportunity for every member of the global work-force." Each day, I work alongside some of the brightest minds in the education and professional networking realms. They are designing products to help everyone learn valuable skills, find jobs, and grow their careers. During my time at LinkedIn, I have been able to meet with many of the leaders in these spaces and I reference them frequently throughout this book.

Third, I also took this one step further to track down and meet with important figures in the world of higher education and business. From these interactions, I was able to glean insights that are not available in any other book.

Lastly, I push myself to be a thought leader in two fields that I believe are directly related to the future of higher education in America: technology and global economics. During my time at UW-Madison, I majored in computer science and economics and have continued to expand my knowledge of these fields post-graduation. You will find applications of my domain knowledge throughout this book.

What is Modern College?

Whenever I tell people the name of my book, the first question they ask is: What does Modern College mean? My answer is that there are multiple layers to its meaning. On a meta level, the name is a nod to the fact that college has changed significantly, not only since the first colleges in the U.S. were founded in the 1600s but in the past decade. What I'm most interested in speaking about is the present-day environment. Today's colleges can no longer be accurately described by staying within the confines of a physical classroom, and success means more than just obtaining a piece of paper. In order to find success, you need to evaluate the college journey from beginning to end and clearly define your goals instead of relying on the system to do it for you. My approach to the book is to speak about college in a way that takes into account the macro factors across education, technology and the workforce in giving students advice that is relevant and actionable.

Because college has changed so much, helping students find success requires a new approach and what better way to teach that approach than through a new type of college? As a college is defined as an educational institution providing higher learning and vocational training, what I am creating is much more than a book, but actually a reflection of what a new type of college could look like. Unlike most colleges today, I believe that the colleges of the future will be much more distributed and open by leveraging all of the cutting-edge technology we have at our disposal.

The platform I am building will utilize more than just in-person lectures and physical books, but also online courses, videos, articles and software tools to help you succeed. While the platform won't be a college on paper, in essence it will represent everything I think colleges will stand for moving forward.

USER GUIDE

How You Should Read this Book

Let's be honest, it's extremely difficult to find time to read books from cover to cover. Humans are living busier lives than ever before and with smartphones and other devices rewiring our brains to desire instant gratification, it's difficult to summon the focus necessary to finish texts longer than a few pages. That's why I wanted to make this book as entertaining and as effortless to read as possible. I started by following the "Rule of Three" and split this book into three distinct sections: **Choose Your Path**, **Get a Degree**, and **Land Your Dream Job**.

In the **Choose Your Path** section, I will break down the true purpose of college and help you find your "why" for attending college. Some of you may find your "why" to be not very compelling or perhaps non-existent. To account for this, I have included a section that gives an overview of the alternatives to a typical 4-year college education. I'll then offer some frameworks that will help you make your decision on pursuing the typical college path or choosing an alternative. As costs are pertinent to the modern college experience, I will discuss some of the basic financial aspects of college to ensure that you are setting yourself up for success far in advance.

For some of you, particularly if you are already enrolled in college, it may be tempting to skip the Choose Your Path section entirely. While I've written the book in a way that allows you to comfortably skip this section, I would highly encourage you to start here, not only because you will undoubtedly find useful advice but it may also instill more confidence in your decision. Did you know that across 4-year postsecondary institutions, **40%** of students either drop out or haven't completed a degree after six years?[1] I was almost one of those students myself. In fact, I even had the paperwork ready to submit during my junior year of college. By reading this section, you can confirm that you've made the right decision or learn the steps you need to take in order to course-correct. While I would love to delve deeper into all of the possible paths both inside and outside of college, I will concentrate all of the advice in the remaining sections of the book to the typical 4-year college education track.

Whether you skip ahead or read through the Choose Your Path section, you will find the **Get a Degree** section waiting for you. In this section, you will find the most pertinent advice needed to successfully navigate the modern college experience. I will cover everything from selecting your major and viewing grades to staying healthy and building the right social network. Many books hit the long tail of the college experience by diving into specifics that don't apply to most students. My approach is different. I adopted Pareto's principle to focus on the 20% of activities and decisions that will define 80% of your college experience. I will also use my own stories and anecdotes to give an unfiltered view of what my college experience was like. These stories are extremely personal and it was difficult for me to find the courage to write about them publicly. But I felt it imperative to include them as they contain important lessons and real examples that you can apply in your own college experience.

Lastly, I tie everything together by discussing how to set yourself up for success post-graduation in the **Land Your Dream Job** section. I address the reality that enrolling in college and graduating with a degree isn't enough to find success. By applying my own experiences and the collective brainpower of my network, I will help you create a plan for embarking on a successful career. This section includes how your major defines your career options, tips on how to succeed at career fairs, and the importance of securing internships early on. It's crucial to read this section no matter if you are still in the college planning stage, you have completed fewer than a semester of classes, or you are nearing graduation. However, reading this section early is best because the decisions you make at the beginning of your college path can alter your chances of finding success later on.

Beyond the Book

Like everything in life, college is constantly evolving. If I had chosen to keep Modern College as just a book, it would have limited the number of students I could reach and the depth to which I could provide relevant advice. Another downside of a book is that it is difficult to update frequently and impossible to revise for those who have already bought physical copies.

That is why I have created a plethora of online videos, articles, and tools for you to reference outside the contents of this book. You can find all of this information at **TheModern-**

College.com. Throughout the book, I will reference specific URLs, which contain more detailed information not included in the book. This supplementary material will be open access and updated regularly. For example, you can find detailed advice on how to craft your resume at **TheModernCollege. com/resume**.

In addition, I have created some proprietary materials, such as online courses and contacts for consultants, including me, which you can find at **TheModernCollege.com/services**.

Lastly, If you enjoy the book and would like to have me speak at your high school, university, or organization, you can access my business contact information on the Modern College website as well.

Modern College for Parents

To any parents who are reading this book, let me start by saying that I am happy to have you here. While I wrote this book with current and prospective college students in mind, I think there is much value in this book for you as well. As I've been preaching in the introduction to the book, college has changed a lot in the past few decades, so much so that it may not even be recognizable in comparison to when you attended. And if you didn't attend college, this book is even more important for you. I know you will find that what I say here will enable you to have important conversations with your son or daughter.

College is a shared journey, especially for those parents who are financing any part of their child's education. For most parents, college will be the largest investment you ever make outside of your house. This can lead to great anxiety in the years leading up to and during college, and even more so after college if your son or daughter does not land a job that enables them to be independent and further their life goals. So please, take the time to read this book before you give it as a gift and have a conversation with your child after they have read it.

Lastly, you may not always like what you read in between the covers of this book and you may even want to shield your son or daughter from the stories I tell about my own experience. However, I highly encourage you not to do this as they certainly won't be shielded from these experiences in college.

For further information and resources specifically for parents please check out **TheModernCollege.com/parents**.

A Few Final Thoughts

Before I began writing this book, I decided to clearly define my principles. The first was to be entirely transparent and frank about my college experience. I wouldn't mask my journey by sugarcoating or hiding my moments of struggle, failure, and humility as I knew that each of these is how I learned the most about myself. The second was that I needed to broaden the scope and evolve my writing so that my advice was applicable beyond the small subset of students who follow my track or attended the same university as I did. This meant that my book would reflect a clear and high quality narrative of overarching concepts and deep dives on key topics. And of course, I wanted to create a piece that is enjoyable to read.

Above all, I sought to write a book that would help others. The experience of college is still fresh in my mind, which means I can still taste the sweet triumphs of success as well as feel the scars from bitter defeats and hard-learned lessons. These experiences, both the good and the bad, made me who I am today.

I picture my current self, handing this book to the younger me as a high school graduation gift or during one of those nights when I was burying my head in a textbook at the library past 3 am. I'd like to imagine that if I had read this book five years ago, I would have had an even better college experience. Unfortunately, time machines don't exist (yet), so all I can do is hand it off to others who are just beginning or still on their college journey. May it serve as a guide book to help you avoid pitfalls and reach heights that you never thought were possible.

Welcome to Modern College.

PART 1:
Choose Your Path

"Two roads diverged in a wood and I—I took the one less traveled by, and that has made all the difference."

—*The Road Not Taken*, Robert Frost

"My mother said to me, 'If you are a soldier, you will become a general. If you are a monk, you will become the Pope.' Instead, I was a painter, and became Picasso."

—Pablo Picasso

T he purpose of this section is to help you answer the seemingly simple question: "Should I attend college?" If you are someone like I was coming out of high school, then this answer may feel like an obvious "yes," primarily because your parents have told you that you don't have a choice. Similarly, if you are already enrolled in college, then this answer may seem like an even more obvious "yes" (this is due to what is known as the *sunk cost fallacy*, which I will discuss in more depth later in Chapter 2). However, let me challenge you to approach this section with an open mind. The fact is that far more people will answer this question with "yes" than is logical. The problem is that most of us have been hard-wired to believe that the only way to find success in today's society is to graduate with a 4-year college degree, while in reality there are numerous other promising paths. Though many people point to individuals such as Steve Jobs or Beyoncé, and say something like, "If *insert wildly successful person* didn't need a college degree, then neither do you," this line of reasoning is unnecessary. I don't need to point to extreme cases to make my point.

According to the former U.S. Deputy Secretary of Education, Anthony Miller, almost 30% of high school graduates with no higher education credentials made more than their peers with associate's or bachelor's degrees in 2013.[2] The implication is that nearly a third of students who are spending the time and money to attend college are finding *less* success than those bypassing college altogether. Also important is the fact that there are close to 14 million middle-skill jobs, a number that is growing, which require more than a high school education but less than a bachelor's degree.[3] These data points indicate that many more students should be answering this question with, "No, I should not attend a 4-year college" than is currently happening.

The cost of answering this question incorrectly is considerable. Not only can it cost you money, given that the students who graduated in 2019 left college with an average debt of $35,359,[4] but the cost in terms of your most precious resource, time, may be even greater. By considering the decision about college from a logical perspective (rather than an emotional one), you will be able to decide on whether college is the right decision for you with confidence. However, before you can do that, let's do a little digging into the history of the U.S. college education system to determine why this question has become a rhetorical one because of the prevailing assumption that everyone should attend college.

A note to the reader:

I know that reading about history can sometimes be boring. But please, if you can be patient for just a few pages of history, I promise to provide more exciting content in the chapters to come.

CHAPTER 1:

The True Purpose of College

College is like a lot of other crucial aspects in our lives. We don't necessarily understand how it became ingrained in our society or why we feel the strong pull to pursue it; we just know that it's something we should care about. However, surprisingly, the current college phenomena is a somewhat recent development. A 4-year college degree wasn't always considered a standard path to success, and there is a growing recognition that it may not be the only path forward in the future either. In order to help you understand this concept, I want to rewind and show you how the purpose of college has changed over time.

Purpose of College Phase One: Train the Wealthy Class and Clergy

The year is 1636, and the first college has just been founded. It takes the name of Harvard in 1639 and its primary purpose is to train clergymen and future leaders of the local community. You could only attend Harvard if you were a young white man from a prestigious family. The cost of taking a son away from the family business or farm was simply too high for most families to absorb. While enrolled in

Harvard, your curriculum would primarily revolve around a slate of liberal arts subjects such as Latin, civic law, and theology. The information was less based on practical knowledge as it was to signal others that you are an intellectual and primed to be a leader. If you were to step outside the realm of Massachusetts, almost no one would know what Harvard was or why it was important to you.

Purpose of College Phase Two: Teach Vocational Skills in High Demand

Fast forward about 200 years and we are standing in front of a library in the middle of the University of Virginia's campus. On the steps is a man who has just finished his presidency, Thomas Jefferson. He speaks to the crowd about his goal to decouple religion from the college experience and to make colleges state-funded so that the less wealthy in society could attend. The basic idea, he states, is to make sure that colleges act as a perfect meritocracy to ensure that the brightest minds in our country are able to learn the practical skills and knowledge they need to advance our society. While his ideas are still far from reality, his words set the stage for major changes in the coming decades.

The first step towards Jefferson's vision becoming a reality occurred when Abraham Lincoln signed the Morrill Land-Grant Act in 1862. As part of this act, states could apply for free land grants from the government, so long as they promoted practical education in areas such as agriculture and mechanic arts. At this point in time, receiving a college education might have been realistic only if you were pursuing a vocation in high demand. That being said, it would still have been perfectly normal and common not to attend college, even if there was a new public college or private institution built in your area. In the year of 1870, only 9,400 bachelor's degrees were awarded.[7] If this seems surprising, you are not alone as the thought that we could have an advanced, well-functioning society without the college experience is entirely foreign to us today. It's difficult to comprehend that this was normal just a few generations ago.

The following table illustrates the growth in college degrees since 1870, and it is likely that the next census will show even further recent growth.[5] Let's look at the trends that led to this growth since the late 1800s.

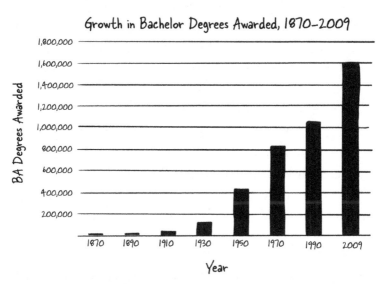

Growth in Bachelor Degrees Awarded, 1870–2009

Source: Bureau of the Census

Purpose of College Phase Three: Drive Military Research and Help Military Members Build a Future after Serving in the War

Our next time jump takes us to 1944, when a federal law stimulated the movement of college to the mainstream of society. The Servicemen's Readjustment Act of 1944, also known as the G.I. Bill, was passed in an effort to support World War II veterans returning from military service. Among its stipulations, the G.I. Bill offered fully covered tuition and living expenses for veterans attending high school, college, or vocational/technical school. While not initially expected to be popular, over 2.2 million vets had taken advantage of the program to enroll in college by 1956. Driven by the momentum of the G.I. Bill, colleges experienced a dramatic increase in bachelor degrees awarded annually from 122,000 in 1930 to more than 827,000 awarded in 1970. By this point, a college education became an expectation.

This trend in college enrollment was seen as a positive trend. As a smart and motivated individual, you could enroll in college at a relatively low cost and start on a positive path upon graduation. The purpose was relatively straightforward and the downside from enrolling was low. In essence, there was a debt-free or low-debt path to the American dream, a perfect meritocracy. So why did this positive trend not continue? Our last few jumps through history will help answer this question.

Purpose of College Phase Four: A Business That Delivered the College Experience and Helped People Land Jobs

Starting in the mid-1970s, the federal government slowly began decreasing financial support for universities. The reason?

Their incentives were no longer aligned. Students began pro-testing things such as military recruitment on campuses and research, which the government had long leaned on universities to drive. However, with independent research facilities spring-ing up, the government grew less reliant on universities to ful-fill this need. These phenomena, along with a number of other variables, caused the federal government to pull large amounts of funding at the same time that states experienced competing needs for reduced revenues, which left many universities in a bind. Some colleges even went under since their operating budgets were reliant on this funding. The colleges that survived began operating like a business, which meant aggressively mar-keting their services and raising their costs to operate in the green. I want you to keep this moment in mind because it was one of the major shifts that led to serious problems with the college system today. We now know that the cost of college is a significant issue, but when the federal and state governments first started pulling funds, the increases in tuition prices did not seem like a big deal. Initially, these cost increases were relatively modest, aligned with inflation and were easily justifiable since a college degree often meant a more successful future.

Over the next few decades, the financial model of uni-versities changed. Competition for students who were pay-ing increasing tuition costs resulted in heavy investments in campuses, from new buildings and residence halls reflecting comfort rather than efficiency, dining facilities that catered to diet and choice preferences, and increased numbers of faculty and support staff for new academic and student life programs. The rise of college athletics (a highly controversial industry) is one example as adding sports became a student recruitment strategy and an increase in specialized social groups, such as with fraternities/sororities, is another because opportunities for joining a social community became another approach to enticing students to one university over another. Universities were no longer just selling the promise of a successful life after college but, also, the experience of a lifetime while in college. And for the most part, this system prevailed into the 2000s. Then the recession happened.

Current Purpose of College: Unclear

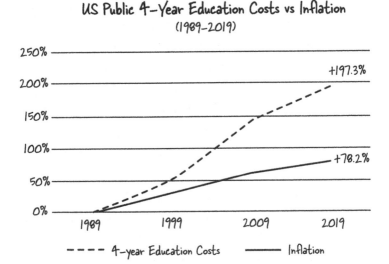

US Public 4-Year Education Costs vs Inflation
(1989-2019)

Source: College Board, US Inflation Calculator

In the year 2008, inexcusable loan practices by large banks led to the housing crisis that ultimately tanked the U.S. and, subsequently, the world economy. One of the immediate repercussions was a reduction in the workforce. As a result, graduates had an extremely difficult time finding employment after graduation and many students resorted to high interest student loans to finance their education. While the economy would bounce back over the next few years, the college model was changed permanently. The cost of college has continued to outpace the cost of inflation to where the cost of attendance has increased 100% more than inflation has increased since 1989.[6] Furthermore, over 50% of young millennials move back to their parents' home for a period of time after graduation.[7] The past decade also saw a rise in terrible campus issues such as sexual assault and underage drinking deaths, which have hurt the image of the classic college experience.

After all of that, we can finally reflect on the present, with you holding this book. There's a lot to unpack from what we just learned, but there are some important nuggets of information that we can glean from the history of college to help guide you on your path moving forward.

CHAPTER 2:

Finding Your Why

It's kind of scary learning about the history of certain things, isn't it? People try to paint a rosy picture all the time, but the reality is that no system is perfect, least of all the college system. As you have learned, the college system has gone through several metamorphoses since its inception, and each one of them defined the purpose of college during different periods of time. Now, unlike in previous generations, the purpose of college is not clear. It's no longer guaranteed that a diploma will land you a great job after graduation, if it ever really did. Similarly, the increasing cost of college has forced students to take out loans that may cancel out any financial gains from employment right out of school.

Whenever you are forced to make a big decision in which the right answer is not clear, it is extremely important that you have all the facts in front of you. To make this as straightforward as possible, I am going to lay out the pros and cons of attending college so that you can determine whether you have a compelling purpose for saying "yes" to college.

So, What is College Good For?

There is truly no other experience in the world like college, largely because it can offer certain experiences that are nearly impossible to have outside of attending college. It is important to start with the things that college is good for because it is a litmus test for whether college is a **requirement** for you or not.

There are certain paths that cannot be reached without a college degree. This means that for some people, college is non-negotiable. Of the many aspects that college is good for, I suggest there are two that can be marked as required, with the rest being nice-to-haves. I've listed these areas below:

- REQUIRED: Fulfill professional requirements
- REQUIRED: Access to key resources
- NICE-TO-HAVE: Establishing independence
- NICE-TO-HAVE: Expanding your network
- NICE-TO-HAVE: A forcing function for learning

I will break each one down and explain why college is one of, or in some cases the *only* way to obtain these things. I will also supplement each with my own experience and learnings. At the end of this section, you may feel that I've painted a very rosy picture of college, and that's ok! College is a truly awesome place and I wouldn't be doing it justice if I didn't start with a strong pitch in its favor.

REQUIRED: Fulfill Professional Requirements

Of all the other benefits, this is the one that I consider to be the defining feature of college. This one aspect could be the sole reason for why you choose to attend college. There are certain opportunities and careers that require at least a 4-year college degree, and in some cases post-secondary education as well. These include, but are not limited to, physicians, nuclear systems engineers, pharmacists, dentists, educational administrators, elementary school teachers; the list goes on. That's also not counting other professions such as many legal and business roles that are nearly impossible to break into without a college degree.

I personally think that this is one of the flaws in our educational system nowadays. There are many professions that require college degrees in order to pursue them. In other words, a piece of paper is almost as important as your skill set and the amount of information you have absorbed in your studies. Though I see this as a flaw, it remains a very real aspect of our present society that we must recognize in order to achieve our professional goals.

Later in this book, I will break down how you can go about defining the professional requirements for a given career path. For now, it's important to just be aware that certain careers will require at least a 4-year degree. If you find yourself homing in on a specific career, do your due diligence and figure out if a college degree is necessary.

REQUIRED: Access to Key Resources

The next benefit is that college will give you access to key resources that you cannot find, or it would be difficult to find, anywhere else. My mind immediately gravitates towards certain STEM research. At my alma mater, resources are available that are vital for pursuing certain careers. For instance, there is a nuclear reactor on campus and a cutting-edge genetics research lab unavailable in many other places in the world for students to learn their craft alongside top scientists.

Beyond equipment and labs, you can interact with some of the best minds in given fields of study. Even with the rise of the internet, there is still nothing that beats stepping into a lecture hall or office to meet with someone who has dedicated their entire life to a subject. This face time allows for a back-and-forth dynamic that simply does not exist to the same degree in online forums.

Once again, the importance of these resources will boil down to what it is you want to study and pursue with your life. It's also important to note that the resources vary widely from university to university. Some will be well funded in certain areas but lacking in others. If key resources are important to you, find out this information before making your decision on which college to attend.

NICE-TO-HAVE: Establishing Independence

It's funny, I spent my entire childhood waiting for independence and when I finally had it, I wished things were simpler again. That's at least how I felt my first few months of college. Sure, I was excited and a little bit relieved after my parents dropped me off on campus, but those initial feelings wore off quickly. Suddenly I was the captain of my own ship, which meant having to operate differently than I ever had before. This is one of the aspects of college that makes it a double-edged sword. With independence comes great power, and as Spiderman fans know, with great power comes great responsibility. That was a lesson I had to learn the hard way many times while in college.

In some ways, my exposure to independence was only a fraction of what others experience in college. I went to an in-state university and home was only an hour and a half drive away. For some of you, your experience will be much different. The moment your parents walk out of your residence hall room, it will mark a much more profound step towards independence as home is a few states away. For others, you may be traveling such far distances that you only get home during semester breaks and your parents won't visit campus until graduation. And yet for others, you may continue to live with your parents or guardians while attending college, and your independence will be built through other means, such as finding affinity groups while your classmates all live in the residence halls and make their friends there. Regardless of your situation, college almost always represents a significant step towards increased independence in life.

Up until college, life's path is pretty uniform for most people. You grow up under the roof of one or more parents or guardians, and you progress through an education system that is quite similar throughout the U.S. You may have had opportunities to learn subjects at a faster pace than your peers but you were likely exposed to a common breadth of educational material and curriculum. The K-12 public education system imposes limits on how deeply you can dive into any one subject area, there is no such thing as majoring in a subject in high school, and any sort of concentrated study is generally done outside of the classroom via clubs or personal interests. For most of us, parents set rules from curfews to diet. This environment eliminates the need for us to make many independent decisions in school or at home.

Then college hits and the paradigm suddenly flips 180 degrees. Whereas before, there was essentially one standard path, college brings a seemingly infinite number of options. There is no one telling you what path you must take. Your counselors will give you a list of required courses but may offer little direction for electives and no direction for how to fill your time outside of class. For the first time in your life, you will have almost complete autonomy over your academic coursework and your lifestyle. While this may appear like a good thing on the surface, it will force you to exercise decision making muscles that may be relatively nascent.

Outside of the changes in your education system, you will (in most cases) be moving out of your parents' house and leaving behind everything they did for you growing up. You will now have to handle all of your daily tasks, such as finding meals and snacks, cleaning up, doing laundry, and scheduling each hour of your day.

Many of us don't realize just how dependent we are on our support systems when growing up. College strips away many of these support mechanisms and forces you to be independent, though within a somewhat controlled environment. While you do have to make some important early decisions, it becomes much easier to function once you've defined your major, daily schedule, and lifestyle habits.

Overall, independence is probably the most hyped up aspect of college and I believe it is for a good reason. If you desire to experience the transition from dependence to independence, within a structured environment where you are surrounded by hundreds or thousands of others your age, then chalk this up under a reason to attend college.

NICE-TO-HAVE: Expanding Your Network

Networking is generally referred to in the professional sense of making connections who can be helpful in promoting your career advancement, and while college does set the foundation for this type of networking, I'd also like to frame it in a few other ways. Beginning with the standard lens for networking, I believe college is a great way to build a foundation for a strong professional network. When you graduate from college, you enter into a closed group of alumni. Someone who graduated from the same university as you will likely have a positive inclination towards helping you. It's just a fact that when feeling a sense of connection with others, it drives our willingness to assist them. With the exception of my first internship, every one of my professional opportunities has been a direct result of my college network.

Different colleges have varying dynamics for how their networks operate. Certain small, private colleges tend to have stronger network effects than others. Classic examples are the Ivy League schools and others like Notre Dame, Georgetown, and Stanford, to name a few. Alumni of these schools have a history of going out of their way to support and advance their own so by attending one of these colleges, you will inherit a very strong and loyal network. Public universities also have their own unique networks that are in many ways just as powerful as these prestigious universities. One reason is that public universities have huge numbers of alumni. If you were to walk into the offices of any large corporation at random, there is a higher likelihood that you will encounter someone from Ohio State, UT-Austin, or Penn State than all of the Ivy League schools combined. By accepting larger classes of undergraduates, public universities have built extensive networks that can open many doors during your career.

Outside of just the professional aspect, college is also an awesome place to build a network of friends. College campuses tend to be more diverse than many geographic areas in the country. Students come from different walks of life and vary considerably in terms of race, ethnicity, hometown, talents, and interests. This is an important aspect of college because you may have spent your childhood in a fairly homogeneous community. A true college experience will allow you to expand your horizons and discover much about yourself. Rather than simply adopting the ideals, values, and pastimes of your childhood community, you can seek out people who actually share your interests, no matter how unique they might be. Did you love playing with computers growing up but were afraid of being labeled a "geek"? Well, you can find plenty of other "geeks" on campus that would be happy to spend their time learning more about computers with you. Have you always wanted to voice a certain opinion but grew up in a community that frowned on the expression of diverse views? College is your opportunity to find friends who share your opinions, or don't and are not afraid to argue with you.

The network effects of college are an important consideration and will pay dividends throughout your lifetime. Both the large-scale network of alumni in the professional world as well as the micro groups of friends you will form on campus are one of the most priceless aspects of college. While one can certainly build a network outside of the college setting, it is often much more difficult and time-consuming. College simplifies and accelerates this process because large numbers of diverse individuals are brought in close contact within and outside of class in ways that enable them to form common bonds.

NICE-TO-HAVE: A Forcing Function for Learning

In my opinion, the most underrated aspect of college is that it forces you to learn. I want you to think back on the number of times you have said that you wanted to learn something but never followed through. What happens in most situations is as follows. You get an initial spike of adrenaline and excitement from the thought of learning something new. You then take an initial step towards starting to learn it. You get a nice upfront return from the initial effort, but then something happens. To become more knowledgeable or skilled, you realize that increasing amounts of effort will be required. This is what is known as a **learning plateau**. Most people think of learning as a linear process; however, this is not the case. The reality is that learning is a never-ending journey filled with long plateaus dispersed with short spikes of improvement. That is why most people give up on learning something new despite their initial excitement. When they encounter the first plateau, they quit since it feels like an impossible journey. The ones who achieve success are those who are able to get past each learning plateau, even embracing these plateaus as part of the learning cycle. Some people are naturally disciplined enough to accomplish this on their own, but I would label these individuals as rare exceptions. Most of us need guidance and support from people who are experts in order to learn something new.

The truth is that no one is inherently great at anything. As Malcolm Gladwell points out in his book *Outliers*, all stories of great success are a direct result of vast amounts of effort put towards improvement. According to the "10,000 hour rule," achieving a mastery level of skill in anything must involve at least 10,000 hours of practice.[8] Countless success stories support its truth. With this rule in mind, the next question becomes: How does one complete so many hours of practice? One way, of course, is through strong self-discipline and willpower. However, given the reality of learning plateaus, this is not realistic for most of us. What a person needs is a strong force to learn more. There are few better forcing functions for learning than college. College will keep you working, honing your skills, and persevering through plateaus. By having a set class schedule, assignments, tests, and a grading system that offers feedback on performance, college ensures that you will push yourself to actually learn what you set out to learn. The irony is that the vast majority of information that you will be taught in college is actually available for free online. However, what you will be missing if you pass up on college is the force to learn.

But, What is College Not Good For?

So now that I have broken down and analyzed some of the things that college is good for, it's important to recognize some of the things that college is not good for. Similar to the good aspects, there are certain flaws inherent in college that may be deciding factors for you. Some of these include:

- High cost
- Serious time commitment
- Locks you into one path (aka The sunk cost fallacy)
- High stress

Again, some of these are more problematic than others. However, it is important to consider all of them when weighing your decision to attend college.

High Cost

College is extremely expensive. For many people, it will be the second biggest investment they will make in their lifetime. But unlike typical investments, the return is often indirect and hard to calculate. Just how expensive is college? Let's take a minute to look at the numbers. According to research by the College Board,[2] the average cost of tuition at a public 4-year college education ranged from $10,440/yr for in-state to $26,820/year for out-of-state in 2019-2020. This number jumps to an average of $36,880/year in tuition at a private college. But tuition is only one of the costs. For both public and private universities, you can expect to pay an additional $16,000/year for room and board, books, supplies, and other expenses. In total, this brings the cost of one year at a 4-year university to be between $26,000–53,980. Spread across four years, the cost of college rises to $104,000–215,920. If you find yourself among the many students who spend five years pursuing your degree, this number could go up to $130,000–269,900 in total costs!

So from a strictly financial point of view, college is a very steep investment. You are essentially making a $100–200K bet that college will give you at least a break-even return on this investment in terms of intangibles (personal fulfillment, knowledge, and experiences) + tangible returns in future earnings potential.

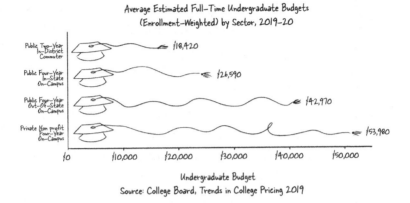

Average Estimated Full-Time Undergraduate Budgets
(Enrollment-Weighted) by Sector, 2019-20

Undergraduate Budget
Source: College Board, Trends in College Pricing 2019

This high cost is only amplified by the financial structures that surround paying for a college education in America. If you're reading this book, it is likely that you will fall under the growing number of students who will take on a sizable amount of debt in order to attend college. As of 2019, close to 54% of college attendees had taken on debt to finance their education.[10] This has led to a collective $1.4 trillion (yes trillion with a t) in outstanding student loan debt in the United States.[11] Currently student loan debt is now the second highest consumer debt category, above both credit cards and auto loans.[12] I could continue to layer on statistics but you get the point. Unless your parents or guardians have saved the money you will need for college, you will be paying off your student loans many years after you graduate.

Let me add one more point. Unless you receive a loan from someone you know, perhaps a family member, the loan is always accompanied by an interest rate. Interest rates are the added fee you pay to borrow the money. While these rates can vary from year-to-year and depend on the source of the loan, you can expect to pay anywhere from 3–7% interest rates on your student loans. Taken over the span of time it takes to pay your loans off, you can expect to have thousands of dollars added to the cost of your already pricey starting cost. There are steps you can take to minimize this burden, which I will cover in the Land Your Dream Job portion of the book.

Overall, there's no denying how much of a factor the price of education can play in deciding on whether or not to go to college. Unfortunately for some, this will be a deciding factor. Later in this chapter, I will provide you with a decision tree to help guide you on whether the cost of education is worth it in your particular case. This decision tree will also help you in comparing the cost of certain universities so that you can factor in these differential costs to the other benefits and drawbacks of each school.

Time Commitment

As of 2017, the average life expectancy for a US citizen was 78.5 years.[13] If you choose to attend college, realize that you will most likely be devoting 4–5 years, or roughly 5–6% of your life, to an education. If you factor in your pre-college education, you will spend close to the first 22 years or ~28% of your life in school. This was my greatest internal dilemma when it came to deciding about college. I kept returning to the question: "Is this the best way that I could be spending my time?" The issue with devoting so much time to college is that it severely limits what you can do during the undergraduate time period. In most cases, you can't begin a professional career or embark on a venture while in college since your education will soak up the bulk of your time. So, there is a giant opportunity cost associated with attending college on top of the financial cost. It is 4–5 years that you could be earning money, gaining experience in the professional world, or growing a business of your own.

To tell you the unvarnished truth, I don't think I optimized my time during the four and a half years that I spent in college. In looking back, I would have been better served spending two years learning in a classroom setting and then heading out into the real world to gain practical knowledge and experience. But I didn't because of the emphasis placed by society on educational milestones. In retrospect, I also know that rushing my education or cutting it short may have limited the options that I currently have. It's difficult to imagine commanding the salary I started with at Intuit without the credentials from a 4-year university.

In the end, it's up to you to gauge if the time commitment is worth it. However, I would not brush off this aspect of college when making your decision. I think that too many people underestimate just how much of their early adulthood they are committing to when signing up for college. As time is one of your most valuable assets, make sure you are spending it appropriately. For most, college will be the most appropriate use of time, but again, not for everyone.

Locks You Into One Path (aka The Sunk Cost Fallacy)

College has a tendency to lock people into one specific path, at least for a period of time. This can be a good thing if you have your heart set on a specific focus for your life as college can be a great mechanism to sharpen this focus and reach your career goals. However, the negative aspect to being locked into one path is that you may have blinders on and fail to consider other paths because so much of your coursework is focused in one area, which is a problem if you initially choose the wrong path.

From the first day of your college orientation, you will already begin to lock yourself into a specific path. Later on, I will tell you about my first day of orientation at the UW-Madison and how it ended up causing me to waste a lot of time and energy. Essentially, I was placed in a panicked situation that ended with choosing a major that wasn't right for me. Unfortunately, I was in denial for a long period of time and spent over two years being too stubborn to admit I was studying the wrong subject. I kept thinking that if I could just grind it out for a few more years, I wouldn't have to deal with the regret of choosing the wrong major.

What I experienced was a strong case of the sunk cost fallacy. According to the sunk cost fallacy, our decisions are influenced by the emotional investments that we accumulate; the more we invest in something, the harder it becomes to abandon. This is because over centuries, the human brain has evolved to focus more on avoiding losses than on maximizing opportunities since it increases the chances of an individual passing on its genes. Think of it this way, each time you invest in an activity that leads to a specific goal, it feels like you are storing away the investment in a vault and it can't be easily transferred to another vault. You feel that if you decide on a different goal, you will lose everything in the old vault and have to start again from scratch. What most of us fail to recognize is the potential upside in switching our focus. The new vault might have the potential to grow much bigger and at a much faster rate. But without being sure of the new vault, it is a struggle to make this jump. We also may not recognize that our investments are much more transferrable than they may appear. While it will never be a perfect carryover, the knowledge and skills we gain in one area can give us momentum in a different area.

It took me two years to course-correct from my original path in college because the longer I spent, the more I felt too invested to back out. I was more terrified of losing the investment I'd made in engineering than I was excited about the potential for switching to a major I was more interested in. College is dangerous because its structure encourages us to fall victim to the sunk cost fallacy. Students are pushed to make really important decisions right away, and these initial decisions have consequences that can actually affect you for your entire life. That's one reason why I advocate for a gap year after high school for some students, which is very common in other parts of the world. At least then, you can spend a year of your life exploring your skill sets and interests before getting locked into a major in college.

High Stress

College is not inherently stressful, though for many students, it does end up being a stressful period in their lives. For those who have not experienced much independence, the move to college can be a shock to the system. The skills required to succeed in college extend beyond the classroom, as each of us must find a way to take care of ourselves in the process. Many students come to college and immediately set their sights on their future without first establishing a stable footing in the present.

There is also a competitive nature built into the college

system that can make it feel like an acutely high-stakes environment. Many universities have exclusive programs that are only available to top performers. This turns the educational setting from one of intellectual enrichment to direct competition among students. The stress that this competition breeds can take a toll on a lot of students, and have ill effects ranging from a decline in mental/physical health as well as wasted time and energy from focusing on the challenge of scoring a high grade more than understanding the subject material.

I firmly believe that stable mental health is important before enrolling in college. If you do not get this under control beforehand, it will be like trying to sprint before you can walk. Unfortunately, colleges tend to focus on the other aspects of their candidates such as how they look on paper, however we must continue to push to amplify the conversation around mental health among college students. Colleges measure vanity metrics such as GPA, but don't really measure important indicators such as stress or happiness levels. Luckily, many universities have begun to recognize these issues and offer mental health services on campus. I will discuss how to find these later on.

High stress and mental health may be factors for why college may not be the right choice for some, at least right now. Spending time focusing on personal health, emotional and physical, before jumping into the competitive and rigorous college environment may make sense for certain individuals.

Putting It All Together

By this point in the book, my hope is that you are more aware of the myriad of different aspects that you should consider when making your college decision. Weighing the pros and cons that I have discussed will be crucial and there is no single right answer for each individual. Not only can different paths each lead to a great outcome but your goals may change over time. It is important that you approach your decision with an open mind and ensure that it is made from a point of logic, not from obligation to your family, desperation to find something else to do, or worry that others will see you as a failure if you don't attend college. Finding your "why" is a critical step in making any decision this big. However, when it feels like you only have one option available to you, it can be tempting to try to fabricate a why out of thin air. If you start with the premise that college is a choice, then you will be more open to other options. In the following pages, you will hear the story of one of my best friends, Ivan Herrada. He said no to college, but was still able to find success.

CHAPTER 3:

The Different Paths

Milwaukee, WI, September 2017

I couldn't tell if it was the drinks I had in the party limo earlier
that evening or the gravity of the moment but regardless of
the culprit, I couldn't help myself as my voice cracked and the
warm tears rolled down my face. My hand trembled as I held
my iPhone in my hand and I tried to read my speech from my
notes app. This was so unlike me. Ever since I was young, I
never had issues with public speaking but, suddenly, my emotions had taken control of me. I paused to clear my throat, as
a room of 100+ people looked on in silence. I glanced to my
right and saw my best friend, Ivan, wave me over to the center
of the wedding table. Slowly, I squeezed past the other chairs

as I made my way across the stage. I stopped next to Ivan's seat and stood next to him and his wife, Caitlin. He patted me on the shoulder and gave me an encouraging head nod. I looked up at the room full of faces watching me, waiting to hear what I said next. I inhaled slowly and caught my breath. I finished the rest of my speech:

I'd like to end my speech with a suggestion for both of you, and that suggestion is to continue to find love in the struggle. That feeling you both have inside of you in this moment, you don't need a wedding event or a room full of people around you to experience it. That love will be present in the weekday nights when work is wearing on you both, but you get to look across the dinner table and see your life partner looking back at you. It will be present during those months where budgets may feel a little tight, but you know you can count on each other to pull through. It will be present 10, 20, and 50 years from now as you both cope with the changes that come with growing older. The love you feel now will always be there, you just need to remember to look for it at all times, even in the midst of adversity.

So to the two people who taught me to find love in the struggle, I toast to you both tonight and to the many years of married life ahead of you. I've loved you both through the good and the bad, and may you continue to do the same with each other.

Congratulations!

After I had raised my arm and downed my drink, I turned and gave Ivan and Caitlin a long hug. I couldn't put into words how proud I was of my best friend. There we were, only a few years removed from high school, and already he was tying the knot with his high school sweetheart. As if getting married wasn't a great enough accomplishment, Ivan had funded most of the wedding by himself on top of buying a car and house that same year.

On the surface, none of this may sound very significant until you consider an interesting fact, Ivan hadn't graduated from college like I had. In fact, our upbringings couldn't have been any more different.

When I first met Ivan, it was in the locker room of our high school. I sat in a corner by myself, listening to rap music off my iPod and staring intently at the soccer ball laying at my feet. The room smelled of sweaty socks and I could hear the laughs of the other guys over my music. It was the first day of soccer tryouts and while most of the other guys were in a light mood, I was all focus. I had made the decision to enroll in Marquette University High School, a private all-boys Jesuit high school that was one of the best in the state and had a price tag on par with some colleges. I had come to Marquette for only two reasons, to increase my chances of getting into an elite university and to compete for soccer state championships. I began eyeing up every guy in the room and my eyes locked onto Ivan from across the room. He stood out because he was one of only three guys in the locker room who wasn't White. He was also more built than just about everyone else and already had a beard. When we stepped onto the field later, I noticed that he was also trying out to be a defender. At the time, I couldn't think of him as anything other than competition. Luckily, we both ended up making the team. I say luckily, because had he not made the team, I would have never met my best friend in high school.

Throughout our high school years, Ivan and I formed a strong bond. At lunch, I would sit with him and his friends. We only had a small percentage of Black and Hispanic students in our entire class, and about half of them sat at our lunch table. Usually I was the only White student with them. I didn't really consider the irony of this dynamic because I just didn't fit in with the other students. Most of them knew each other from private primary schools and lived in towns that were 30-45 minutes away from me. While they would talk about their experiences at country clubs and expensive vacations, I was exposed to very different conversations at my lunch table.

Ivan didn't have the same opportunities I did. Each day he would have to wake up earlier and catch the public bus in order to get to school. He was also there on a scholarship, which required him to do extra tasks around the school. But most of the time, our lives didn't feel that different.

Beginning senior year, things began to change. Ivan's parents were divorcing and his dad was moving back to Mexico. He was going to lose his childhood home and aside from moving in with his mom, he would have to be completely financially independent. While I was toiling over college admissions and planning to leave home in a few months, Ivan was just trying to stay afloat.

I don't remember when we specifically had the conversation but at some point, Ivan told me that he would not be pursuing a typical 4-year college degree. I was shocked. "Can't you just take out loans or something?" I said to him. He shook his head and tried to explain to me his situation. I struggled to comprehend his point of view. We had attended a college prep school, one of the best in the entire state, and he wasn't even going to go to college? I didn't push it since I understood his situation, but I still felt badly for him. At the end of our senior year, the high school newspaper published a map of the U.S. and a pin for where every student in our class was going. In our class of 250+ students, almost all had their names next to a big-name school. I scanned the map and looked for trends. Of course, there was a huge chunk of students like me who would be attending the University of Wisconsin-Madison. A good chunk of students had even gotten into Ivy League schools, which wasn't surprising considering the *average* ACT in our class had been a 28 of 36, which is considered a very high score. Eventually, I got to the end of the list and saw a category titled "Other." There were only five students in that list; one of them was Ivan.

Over the next few years, while I partied in college and buried my nose in books, Ivan got to work. He was able to land a job in one of the trades, where he became an insulator who worked in the most grueling weather conditions in Wisconsin. Every day, he woke up at 4 am and drove to his job. In winter, he wore three layers so he could withstand the below zero temperatures, and in summer he sweated through his shirt as he dealt with the notoriously humid Wisconsin weather. It was in the afternoons that he got to work on his passions. Ivan was an artist by nature and while he knew it wasn't enough to sustain him financially in the short term, he didn't let his dreams die. He started multiple side projects, including a successful clothing brand and photography business with his partner Caitlin. While Ivan didn't have a college education, he did learn a few crucial skills on his own including online marketing & SEO, graphic design, and the basics of finance. Furthermore, his creative mindset, disciplined schedule and high tolerance for discomfort allowed him to advance.

When I finally made it to my college graduation, Ivan and Caitlin were the only two people outside of my family that made the trip to my campus. Ivan may not have had a college degree on that day, but he was as successful as anyone walking across the stage. In short, Ivan had found another path.

I decided to include the story of my friendship with Ivan in order to lend a perspective that I lacked. Up until I watched Ivan pursue a different route, I genuinely didn't realize that going to college was a choice and there could be more than one path to success. That is why I felt it was important to help others discover the other options available to them outside of college. I cover a few of these in this section. The goal isn't to be comprehensive in my analysis but rather to help you identify opportunities in areas you might not have considered before.

Alternative Path: Self-Employment

Every day, millions of people wake up and go to work for themselves. While this is not something that I have personally done, I have nothing but respect for people who have chosen this path. It can be challenging to imagine a future in which you work for yourself because our K-12 education system doesn't really teach the skills or mindset necessary to pursue this route.

There are many ways in which to start working for yourself, so it is difficult to address each one individually. However, there are frameworks that can guide your thinking if self-employment is right for you. Let me start by defining what I consider to be the two main types of self-employment:

1. Partial self-employment through an existing platform
2. Creating and running a unique endeavor entirely on your own

Some examples of jobs in bucket 1 are in the gig-economy space. These include driving for Lyft or Uber, renting your property on Airbnb, or doing tasks for a fee such as freelance writing on Fiverr or furniture movement on TaskRabbit. I consider these to be forms of partial self-employment because they exist on platforms that obfuscate some of the details that accompany traditional self-employment. For instance, Lyft and Uber solve the customer sourcing, marketing, and even many of the accounting aspects. All you have to do is provide your time, property, and driving ability. It is easier than ever to find roles in the gig-economy space and they will likely be around for the foreseeable future. There are a lot of benefits to be had from gig economy roles, such as flexibility over your schedule and location, plus low barriers to entry. However, there are also downsides to the gig economy. For starters, all of these roles are temporary and do not carry long-term growth prospects. None of these platforms offer any equity to their base of gig workers, so any growth these platforms realize go to the people actually building and running the platform. Furthermore, a lot of these platforms are under scrutiny for their practices. As of now, they consider the majority of their workers to be independent contractors, which means that they do not provide the benefits that exist in a typical employee-employer agreement, such as health insurance. Lastly, the skill sets you gain from these jobs aren't necessarily transferable. My advice in regards to gig economy jobs is that they are a good stop-gap but should not be considered a long term solution. If you feel that you need time to map out your future path, then these jobs are perfect because they provide you with flexibility and just enough money to keep you afloat.

There are also other types of self-employment that I feel are more legitimate because they offer long-term growth and security. I've listed some of these based on volume in the chart below. The data was pulled from the Bureau of Labor Statistics and organized by SmartAsset.com[14].

The degree of independence in each of these roles can vary. For some of the roles listed above, there are companies that will cover certain aspects of the business while letting you control others. To give an example, many people begin their careers in real estate by joining an existing firm. After spending a sufficient amount of time building up their skills and network, they can choose to branch off and start a real estate firm on their own.

Some people choose to immediately jump to this step. They may do it in one of the ways I have discussed or in a theoretically infinite amount of other ways. There isn't a single formula for starting your own venture; however, there are some universal truths that can guide your thinking. The most important thing is to solve a real problem or need for a specific subset of the population. The problem should be important enough that people are willing to pay you for a product or

TOP 15 JOBS FOR SELF-EMPLOYMENT
Ranked By Projected Job Openings

Rank	Job	Percent Self-Employed	Median Income	Projected Workforce Growth	Projected Job Openings
1	Construction Laborers	25.7 %	$31,090	12.7 %	378,600
2	Management Analysts	19.1 %	$80,880	13.6 %	208,500
3	Carpenters	33.6 %	$40,820	6.4 %	169,100
4	Farmers and Ranchers	70.7 %	$68,050	-1.9 %	158,400
5	Personal Financial Advisors	20.2 %	$81,060	29.6 %	136,400
6	Self-Enrichment Education Teachers	21.5 %	$36,020	15.4 %	119,200
7	Writers and Editors	35.5 %	$59,710	0.7 %	85,700
8	Actors, Producers, and Directors	19.8 %	$59,560	9.2 %	84,500
9	Construction & Maintenance Painters	41.3 %	$35,950	7.4 %	83,900
10	Property and Real Estate Managers	43.7 %	$54,270	8.1 %	79,900
11	Food Service Managers	34.2 %	$48,560	5.1 %	77,100
12	Construction Managers	38.0 %	$85,630	4.8 %	70,100
13	Massage Therapists	47.7 %	$37,180	21.6 %	49,000
14	Artists and Related Workers	53.9 %	$65,860	3.5 %	42,000
15	Roofers	18.6 %	$35,760	12.8 %	34,700

* Workforce growth and job openings are projected by the
Bureau of Labor statistics through 2024

Source: SmartAsset.com

service that solves that problem. After you have defined these problems, the key is to figure out which product or service you have the ability to create solutions for.

Alternative Path: The Trades

The next path is the "Trades." Generally speaking, the Trades refers to skilled jobs such as electricians, plumbers, and construction managers, among others. In many ways, the Trades have been painted as unsexy jobs that should not be pursued because they offer no prestige. Mike Rowe talks a great deal about the problems with this perception of skilled blue collar jobs and even created a foundation, the Mike Rowe Works Foundation[15], that is committed to changing the narrative about the Trades.

The reality is that this country was built by people who work in the Trades and it remains a solid life path. If you're someone who has brushed this career path off in the past, here are a few reasons you may want to reconsider.

For starters, the overall cost/benefit of pursuing this path could work out much better for you than pursuing a 4-year degree. Second, the barriers to entry are relatively low. There aren't too many credentials needed to enter and the cost of mandatory training is low in comparison to a bachelor's degree. Lastly, these jobs are always in demand and nearly impossible to outsource, ensuring that you will likely have job security during your working lifetime. I would recommend doing further research if this is a path you are interested in to determine how to gain the training needed for a specific trade in which you have an interest and talent, but below is a high-level overview of the steps you need to take to pursue this path for many of the trades.

1. Obtain your high school diploma (necessary for most, if not all trade jobs).
2. Attend a technical or vocational school. Usually this will only take 1–2 years and the curriculum will center around knowledge directly related to the skills you will need in the job.
3. Obtain an apprenticeship. Most of the time, apprenticeships are set up through local unions.
4. Spend 2–5 years as an apprentice, which will involve being paid for on-the-job training along with some relatively brief classroom work.
5. After completing a minimum amount of apprenticeship hours and passing tests of your knowledge and skills, you will become a Journeyman, which will come with a bump in pay.
6. If you choose, you can then complete further training to become a Master Tradesman, which comes with an increase in pay and scope of role.

In terms of financials, the Trades are an overall solid option. They usually only cost a few thousand dollars to pursue and according to employee data sourced by Indeed, they can pay between $45,760-$122,573 per year,[16] depending on your years of experience. If you are really ambitious, you can also take your skills and start your own firm, which can lead to even higher levels of income. This is a really nice financial outlook, especially when you consider how many college students now graduate with serious debt and much bleaker earning prospects.

To summarize, the Trades are an extremely underrated path that most people overlook. Despite the abundant availability of jobs in these fields and the critical role they play in our society, many remain vacant each year. Perhaps you might be one of the people that will help fill this need.

Alternative Path: Online Education

The next option has both some similarities and major differences between the Trades, and that is pursuing some form of online education. Similar to the Trades, online education strips away many parts of the traditional college experience and focuses on practical knowledge and skills. Also like the Trades, the cost of online education tends to be lower than a brick-and-mortar college education because of the lower overhead costs from not needing to support physical infrastructure and the ability to reach more students with fewer professors. However, where they differ is in their areas of focus.

Online education tends to be best suited to those pursuing white collar professions, especially those that require extensive use of computers or software. The good news is that low cost hardware and software advances such as the internet have made it so that almost any person in America can pursue an online education from any place. Nearly any undergraduate major at a traditional 4-year college can be pursued fully online. The unfortunate news is that not all online programs offer a high-quality education. In order to help you separate the signal from the noise, I've done a breakdown of the different categories of online learning and how you can pursue each one of them. However, I also encourage you to do your own due diligence before committing to a program if you decide to go this route.

Online Learning Platforms

Over the past decade or so, a number of large online learning platforms have emerged. These platforms are used to teach skills and knowledge across a variety of fields. Some of these platforms include certifications that can be used to signal your abilities and land professional opportunities.

There are subtle differences in terms of what services you can expect to find on each platform. Some platforms are strictly focused on providing courses or content at a relatively low cost. While they offer plenty of content, they tend to be less institutionally focused. Basically, they provide online learning content but not necessarily certifications or even a set structure. Examples of these platforms include Udemy, LinkedIn Learning, Khan Academy, and Skillshare, among others. These platforms are nice places to learn skills but they have limitations. For starters, there aren't strong forcing functions in place to keep you accountable and moving forward. When coupled with a modest cost, you may find that you aren't incentivized to put forth the self-discipline and effort required to pursue these programs. They also don't focus as much on certifications or degrees, which may make it difficult to leverage the platform to secure a standard corporate job. These platforms are best suited for those looking to become freelancers or build upon skill sets while working in an existing job.

Some online learning platforms have leaned into providing credentials and a structured environment. Platforms such as Coursera and Udacity have put formal programs in place and are a better fit for some students. You can pay to take an online course with mandatory lectures, assignments, and virtual interactions with classmates. At the end of the courses, you may receive a certification from the program. Over the years, these certifications have grown to carry more value in various industries and can sometimes act as a legitimate credential for landing a job.

Coding Boot Camps

Another specific type of online learning that has grown in popularity is coding boot camps. With a massive demand for software and IT type workers, online coding boot camps have sprung up to help educate mass numbers of participants. Coding boot camps can run anywhere from a few months to two years, depending on what skill sets you are seeking to learn. These bootcamps are usually much cheaper than a traditional university degree (~$12K on average),[17] and tend to have decent job placement and earning potential upon completion.

Some coding boot camps are hybrid programs in that they include online and face-to-face training. This may be helpful for those who need more hands-on support or accountability to finish the program.

Another type of program that is similar to a boot camp is the one championed by Lambda School. What makes Lambda School a unique model is that no fees are charged upfront; instead you pay 17% of your income for two years once you begin earning at least $50K annually.[18]

Overall, coding boot camps or any type of online technical training can be a great option due to the fairly low entry requirements, reasonable cost, and abundance of jobs in this field. However, there are a few words of caution I would give to anyone looking to pursue this path. The first is that these types of jobs are not for everyone. While these jobs are painted to be sexy high-paying jobs, some of these roles can vary from being extremely mentally challenging to involving mundane or repetitive work. Another is that the current tech supply versus demand asymmetry may not last forever. As the influx of tech talent to the labor market increases, this increased supply could eventually result in lower wages and greater competition not only for the best jobs, but also those on the lower end of the tech skill spectrum.

Online Universities

The last option for online education is pursuing a formal degree program from an accredited university. This path may make more sense for those who still want a 2- or 4-year education and the name recognition of a prominent university while keeping the flexibility and lower costs that an online education can provide.

One of my friends, Kasey Altman, completed her degree via Penn State University's World Campus program while traveling all around the world. I actually met Kasey at a hostel in Cartagena, Colombia. She was taking an online course while in Cartagena, and the program was not only accredited but carried the prestige of Penn State. Upon graduation, the name recognition of Penn State helped her land a full-time role at a top tech startup in New York City less than three months after she completed the program.

Many universities have been expanding their online presence in response to changes in society, such as the need for flexibility to accommodate individuals with work and family responsibilities, and the increasing quality of online education. While you lose some of the aspects of a traditional college experience, there are certainly tremendous benefits to earning a degree from a highly reputable university via an online medium. You can find the names of some universities that currently offer online degrees at guidetoonlineschools.com.

Alternative Path: Community College

If you are still leaning towards a traditional college degree but aren't totally committed, then community college may be a good option for you. A community college can open up a number of different doors, depending on what you are seeking.

For those looking to eventually attend a 4-year university, community college can provide a clear path. The community college curriculum offers the general education requirements and prerequisites to many majors for most 4-year institutions. If you succeed at community college, the transition is usually smooth. Most, if not all, of the courses you satisfactorily complete will transfer to your 4-year degree, which can save you money as community college tuition is quite low.

If you aren't looking for a 4-year degree or are still unsure, community college can be a good way to complete your formal education at a very reasonable price. Community colleges offer associate degrees, certificates, and technical training. Programs in the health professions, such as nursing, are some of the most popular and graduates are in great demand. Depending on your goals, community college may be the right option for you.

The good news is that community colleges are a relatively low risk path to pursue. Public community colleges only cost around $4,811 per year on average*, which is much lower than most 4-year institutions.[19] Another benefit is that if you pursue a two-year program, you won't lose much time if the path doesn't work for you.

*Cost is based on in-state tuition. Out of state rises to $8,584.

Alternative Path: Gap Year

Another path that isn't talked about nearly enough in the United States, but is popular in other countries, is the idea of taking a gap year. During a gap year, you can pursue a variety of activities including working a job, traveling, volunteering locally, or joining AmeriCorps Vista, City Year, or Peace Corps. This will also buy you time to explore your interests and reflect on future options.

The data shows that taking a gap year can be a great choice for some people. For instance, 90% of students who originally intended to go to college before their gap year do enroll afterwards. Furthermore, the extra time spent exploring one's interest can pay dividends in the classroom since 60% of students who took a gap year said that it helped them decide what subject to study in college and 66% also said they took their classwork more seriously when they did enroll.[20]

A gap year can also be a good idea in general for many young adults since the human mind continues to develop into its 20s. This extra brain development might help you make better decisions while in school and increase your chances of having success in life as a result.

Gap Year Stats

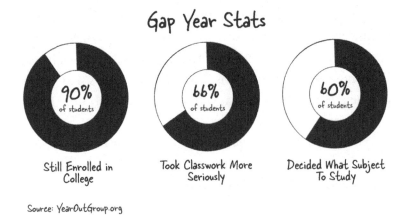

90% of students
Still Enrolled in College

66% of students
Took Classwork More Seriously

60% of students
Decided What Subject To Study

Source: YearOutGroup.org

Other Alternative Paths

What if you still haven't seen a path that appears right for you? The good news is that there are potentially an infinite number of other paths that you can take.

One of these is the military, where you will receive training that you can use not only during your service but when you complete your term of service. Another could be finding some type of job that I didn't list out above. The possibilities are truly endless.

Above all, though, the key is to eventually choose a path. The reality is that no path is set in stone and you can always change course later. Your worst enemy coming out of high school is inertia or doing nothing out of fear. I know it's easier said than done but I promise that if you choose a path and work hard, it will be a lot easier to find success moving forward. To help you choose that path, I will next offer some helpful tips for making your decision.

CHAPTER 4:

Making Your Decision

My first job out of college, I took a role as Associate Product Manager at Intuit in Silicon Valley. During my time there, I had the opportunity to work directly with Intuit's founder, Scott Cook. For those who don't know, Intuit is the maker of financial software including the extremely popular TurboTax, Quickbooks, and Mint software products. One thing that I learned from Scott was how to make difficult decisions when there is a lot riding on them. What he taught me was to apply frameworks to guide your thinking. Scott has created frameworks for how to interview users, build new products, and improve business practices. It was Scott who inspired me to create frameworks for other areas of life.

One framework I decided to create was around deciding whether or not you should attend college. Below I present the steps in the framework. By the end of the section, you should have the tools you need to either confirm your existing plan or change your course.

College Decision Framework

Step 1: Begin with the End in Mind

Ask yourself, where do I want to be in 5–7 years? Select 2–3 jobs/professions you could envision as right for you. Separately, list 2–3 other life factors (such as, living in a warm climate, time frame to start working professionally, making more than $X, carrying less than $Y in debt). Don't worry if the lists are not perfect; however, the more specific, the better.

Determine what it would take to achieve success in each one. For example, if you want to be a software engineer at Google, break down the steps to get there. If it requires you to have a certain degree or set of skills, you will need to select a university or program that offers these.

Highlight the steps that are shared between multiple goals. This will be important for making the decision.

Note that the purpose of this step isn't to force you to make serious life decisions on the spot but rather to think about the end-to-end process that will lead to finding success in the future.

It's also important to remember that what you want in life may change over time. You need to learn how to be reflective, follow the process of defining and redefining your goals, and recognize what is needed to achieve them.

Step 2: Run Cost-Benefit Analyses

For each of the 2–3 options you have listed, run a quick cost-benefit analysis of each one. That is, what would it cost to achieve your goal and once you reach it, how much benefit will it provide in terms of earnings and lifestyle?

Focus your cost-benefit analysis on the average for every step along the way. For instance, if you want to become a physician, take the average amount of years it takes to accomplish and multiply it by the average cost of an undergraduate education and medical school. Then find the average amount a physician in your field earns and figure out how long it will take you to break even in terms of your investment.

If you find yourself fortunate enough to have your tuition covered by your parents, you should still perform this step. Consider involving them in this cost breakdown step so everyone is aware of the financial sacrifice they will be making.

Many people will tell you to just blindly follow your passion instead of considering the cost-benefit analysis of various life paths; however there is considerable danger in doing this. Famed Silicon Valley investor and startup founder Naval Ravikant has put forward an important perspective. He states that you should focus on achieving financial stability first and pursuing your passions after. In other words, it's much easier to follow through on your goals if you don't have to worry about other problems that money can eliminate.[21]

The reason that it's easier to pursue our passions when we are already in a stable position is that we have limited brain power to expend in a given day. In his book, *Thinking Fast and Slow*,[22] Daniel Kahneman describes the two systems that our mind utilizes. System 1 is for reactionary things like breathing or driving on an empty road. They require very little effort from our brain to complete. However, System 2 activities, such as trying to multiply 17x24, require much more brainpower. The problem with pursuing a path with a negative financial outcome is that it means you will likely divert a lot of energy to System 2 activities that are necessary to survive. All of this brain energy that is put into survival activities is energy that is not being put into achieving your goals.

I'm not suggesting you should run to investment banking as a career because it has a positive payout. However I do want you to be aware of the implications of the paths you are considering. If you choose a path with a high probability of a negative financial return, it may prevent you from achieving some of the things you listed in step 1. This approach can help you filter out some of the career paths you are considering. In general, I suggest avoiding paths with negative financial returns unless you have a compelling reason, such as possessing a unique skillset or connections that will enable you to be a positive outlier.

Step 3: Binary College Decision Tree

Because this is a book on college, the final step is to figure out how much of the book actually applies to you. I've devoted a large chunk of this first section to exploring alternative options to college. You now know that there is more than one way to find success, and that pursuing a 4-year college degree is just one of many paths.

I want to now return to the question that I posed at the beginning of this section. Should YOU be attending college? While this is a big decision, it isn't necessarily a permanent one. You can choose to say no to college initially and change your mind at a later date. Likewise, you can enroll in college and later step out if your outlook changes. However, you do eventually need to make a clear yes or no decision on college and the decision tree below should assist you.

College Decision Tree

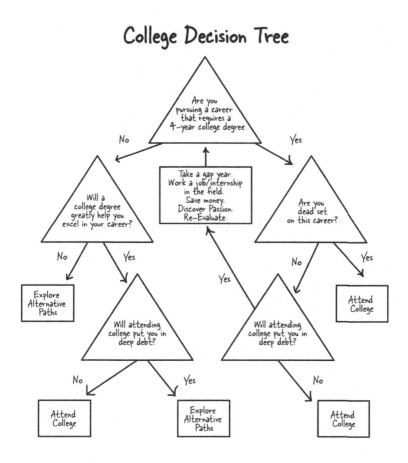

A few things to note when using this tree:

If you aren't completely set on a single career track, try running it for your top 2–3.

If you receive different answers for different paths, think hard about how set you are on any of the paths that output "Yes" as an answer. If you are still split, it might be a good sign that you need to take a gap year until the answer becomes more clear. Alternatively, see which ones bubble to the top after deep reflection. You may need to take a leap of faith on one.

If you used averages for your cost-benefit calculations but have a very specific college in mind, run the actual numbers and see if the decision tree output shows differences.

This tree may seem a little cold and overly calculating. However, it forces you to make a decision based on data and logic.

Choosing and Applying to Colleges

I made an intentional decision not to delve too deeply into the college selection and admission process in this book. I have provided materials online that delve into this topic in greater detail, which you can find at **TheModernCollege. com/admissions**. This subject can become very detailed and complex, and may not be applicable to everyone reading this book. That being said, I do have a few important things to say.

When it comes to choosing which colleges to apply to, it is important to reference the notes you created as part of your decision process on whether to attend college at all. You need to approach college with a holistic, end-to-end mind-set. The life you want to be living in a few years is inherently linked to the job you land after graduation. And the job you land after graduation is inherently linked to what you learn through your major and extracurriculars. And the majors and extracurriculars available to you are inherently linked to the college that you attend. All of this is to say that whatever colleges you apply to should align with your goals a few years after graduation.

For every life goal that you have, you should run a quick mental simulation and see if there are gaps that will arise from attending any of the colleges that interest you. For example, if one of your life goals is to design airplanes at Boeing after graduation, then it doesn't make sense to apply to a small liberal arts college with no engineering program. Likewise, if you're dead set on a major that you know will not result in a career with high earning prospects, then it's probably not a good idea to apply to a college with such high tuition that you will end up buried in debt. These things may sound obvious but prospective students can get so wrapped up in the names of colleges that they forget to check on how those colleges will actually position them for life after graduation.

I will make one exception to this advice, which is that there are a handful of colleges for which the brand recognition alone can be the deciding factor for attending. NYU Professor and entrepreneur, Scott Galloway, refers to these as the "15 Top 10 universities,"[23] which are the most prestigious and consistently ranked in top 10 college lists. If you get into Harvard or Stanford, then you can basically throw away the college decision framework and have confidence that you will find a good path if you attend. However, for every single university outside this tight circle this does not hold true. Don't drink the kool aid that every university pitches which is that they are worthy of attending based on name recognition alone. It isn't true for my alma mater, and it's not true for the other 99.8% of colleges out there either.

This exercise will ensure that you are not only applying to colleges you are excited about attending but these colleges will also be right in practical ways including cost and your life goals. Though the marginal costs in terms of time and money of applying to each additional college are modest, my advice is to keep the number of applications to no less than five and not more than ten. By submitting applications within this range, you reduce the chances of not getting into any college (though you should always apply to at least one safety school), while also making sure you're not overwhelmed with too many options if you are accepted at every school.

Owning Your Decision

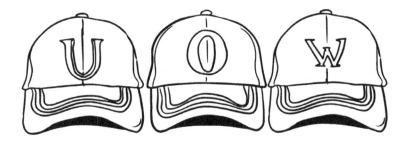

Milwaukee, WI, 2012

I laid out the offer letters in front of me on our old wooden kitchen table. I scanned over them and nodded in approval. I had applied to seven colleges and been accepted to all of them. I imagined that my decision would be more dramatic. I wanted it to be like the 4-star high school athletes making their decision on which scholarship offer to accept. The different college hats would be stacked out in front and the room would crackle with excitement as I reached for my choice, put it on in front of the cameras, and smiled wide.

At the very least I expected there to be a discussion but,

in reality, the decision had been made for me. Out of all seven universities, the University of Wisconsin-Madison offered the best combination of prestige, curriculum, and price by a long shot. With an in-state tuition of around $9,000, UW-Madison was more than $40,000 per year cheaper than some of the other schools and even when their financial aid packages were considered, the cost differential was great.

What my parents were having a hard time comprehending was just how badly I wanted to leave the state. In many ways, high school had been rough for me. During my freshman year, my grandfather Joe "Poppy" Valaitis passed away from cancer. We were extremely close and he had pushed hard for me to attend MUHS. In our last conversation, he told me that I was special and that I needed to help make a name for our family. I took those words to heart.

Then my sophomore year, I hit another roadblock. It was a week after soccer season had ended and I was trying to play catch up in band class. I played tenor saxophone and had a solo in the upcoming jazz concert. The week before the concert, I was in my dad's office in a far corner of our house, trying to practice my solo at 1 am without waking up my family. At one point, it became difficult to make sounds come out of the saxophone. I figured I was just worn out so I packed up my saxophone and went to sleep. The next day, I was struggling to breath. I couldn't even make it up a flight of stairs without being winded. I knew something was off but I wasn't sure what exactly. I went to see my primary doctor that afternoon, figuring it was some minor ailment. She sent me to get an x-ray "just as a precaution." Three hours later, I heard the phone ring and I picked it up from upstairs. My mom had already answered from the home phone downstairs so I just sat there and listened. "You need to get Alex to the hospital immediately. His lung has collapsed and he's in serious danger." I felt a cold sweat come over my body as I hung up the phone in disbelief. Two surgeries and 14 days later I was released from the hospital. I had experienced what was called a "spontaneous pneumothorax," in which a small hole had formed in my lung. The condition had been present for some time but it was the pressure from playing the saxophone that finally turned it into a crisis. One of the worst memories from that year was taking a pre-calculus exam in the hospital and finding myself setting down my pencil and pressing the plastic yellow button on the hospital controller that dispensed my morphine drip.

If sophomore year was difficult on a physical level, it was senior year that really did me in on a mental level. The year started off terribly, when I was the last one cut from the varsity soccer team. The failure of my soccer endeavors seemed to bleed into all areas of my life and made me question everything. What had all these years of hard work been for? While many of my public school friends had fun on weekdays and rarely did more than 1-2 hours of homework a night, I had reduced my social life to do 4-5 hours of homework each night in order to keep up. Yet, somehow, I was going to end up at the same university as many of them?

By the time I was making a decision on college, I was burnt out. I was tired of operating in hyper-competitive environments. I was tired of spending all of my free time with my nose buried in books. And I was definitely done trying to please others. All I wanted was to go somewhere new and focus on having fun for a change.

I had a lot of arguments with my parents during the final few months of my senior year and into summer. I rebelled in different ways. Whether it was getting my ears pierced or underage drinking, I was continually finding new ways to upset and exasperate them.

I love my parents, but by the end of summer it became clear that it was time for me to move out and head to college. Externally, I acted excited to be attending UW-Madison but deep down, my heart wasn't in it yet.

It's not easy for me to discuss this stage of my college journey. I wish the process had been smoother and that I had a brighter story to tell, but the truth is that I was extremely lost during this period of time. I never really made an explicit decision to attend college, it just happened. My parents paid the tuition, room, and board, I packed up my car at the end of summer, and suddenly I was on my way.

I was fortunate to be in a position where I didn't need to think about this decision, and being on autopilot didn't hurt me. However, this will not be the case for many of you. This decision will be one that you must think long and hard about or, at the very least, put more effort into than I did. While I didn't practice what I preached in this section, I believe I have provided the necessary information to make an informed decision.

In Part 1, you learned:
- Why college exists
- What college is and isn't good for
- Alternative paths to college
- How to make a yes/no decision on college
- Advice for deciding which college to attend

These are necessary steps to answering the question I posed at the beginning: "Should I attend college?" Hopefully you now have your answer. For those who answered "No," I have discussed other paths you can follow. For those of you who answered "Yes," you should now feel confident about your decision. In Part 2, I will offer advice that will ensure you maximize your 4-6 years of college and set yourself up for success after graduation.

PART 2:
Get a Degree

"Education is not just about going to school and getting a degree. It's about widening your knowledge and absorbing the truth about life."

— Shankutala Devi

"I can't tell you what I learned from school, but I could tell you a story or two."

— Asher Roth, I Love College

I can still remember the rush of air and clank of metal as the door closed and my parents left my dorm room. It's hard to describe that moment, the one in which you encounter true freedom for the first time. I remember just sitting there and absorbing it all. It was a weird mix of joy, fear, sadness, and excitement all at the same time.

So much of my life had been centered around making it to this exact position and now that it was finally here, I wasn't sure what to make of it. For a few brief minutes, I launched into a deep state of contemplation. "I've finally made it," I thought to myself, "Now what?" Before I could figure out my entire life while lounging on my couch, my roommate burst into the room with his parents carrying a beer pong table and a 12-pack. "Welcome week, let's go baby!" he yelled. I laughed and jumped up to greet him and his parents.

As crazy as it sounds, I feel like my life entered light speed from that day until I walked across the stage for college graduation. Sure, there were moments in my four and a half years of college in which I reflected deeply. However, I could never quite seem to piece together a holistic picture. Luckily for me, I was able to figure things out on the fly and I ultimately landed in a great spot. But the truth is that I am very fortunate things didn't go sideways for me along the way.

What I will explain in this section is everything that I learned from the moment my parents left me alone in my college dorm, to the day I walked across the stage for graduation.

The Three Things that Matter in College

It's hard to recount my entire college experience in just a few sections of a book, but when you boil things down to the essentials, my advice is straightforward. You see, there are only three things that truly matter in college. This might sound like an oversimplification but if you get these three things right, everything else will fall into place.

What you learn

Who you surround yourself with

What you do

Now your first reaction to this list is probably, no sh*t Sherlock, this is literally 100% coverage of college! But we need to go one click deeper into what I mean about each of these. For each, there are three essential aspects.

What You Learn

- What your major is
- How you learn
- Extracurricular activities

Who You Surround Yourself With

- Who you live with
- How you go about networking and, once again
- Extracurricular activities

What You Do

- Getting good enough grades
- Staying out of trouble
- Taking care of yourself

That's all there is to it. Three essential buckets, each with three corresponding areas of focus, for a total of nine things to get right in order to be successful in college. Seems simple? I'll spend the next few chapters making sure it actually is.

CHAPTER 5:

What You Learn

Make no mistake about it, knowledge is one of the most powerful tools you can acquire in life. It also happens to be one of the primary reasons for why you should enroll in college, the pursuit of more knowledge. Two key aspects of the learning process involve **what you learn** and **how you learn**. The focus of this chapter will be on what you learn.

There has never been an easier time in the history of the world to acquire new knowledge. With the advent of the internet, the answer to any question is only a few keystrokes away. However, with this great power comes complications. For starters, it has become more difficult to separate signals from noise, or the valuable from the worthless. While the internet has made it easier to gain knowledge, it has also made it much simpler to create and distribute content. This has led to an influx of low quality content as well as false information, which can be mistaken for truth if you are not careful. Furthermore, the vast amount of information on the internet has made it more difficult to prioritize which information we need or want to obtain.

The good news is that college is a great way to concentrate

on what you want to learn and make sure that you are in an environment that will help you separate the important from the unimportant and facts from falsehoods. Also, as much as students may complain about grades, they serve as a great forcing function for learning. College makes you put a lot of skin in the game and in turn, drives learning at a deep level in whatever it is you want to pursue.

This is a great segue to the topic of choosing your major. Ultimately, much of what you learn in college will connect to your major, so it is a natural starting place.

Choosing Your College Major

No decision you make in college will be more important than your decision on which major to pursue. Despite this fact, most students enter college woefully unprepared to select a major that actually suits them and their future interests. I believe the reason is because there is a disconnect between high schools and universities. On the one side, universities expect students to arrive knowing exactly what they want to study. On the other side, high schools focus on getting you into college and then wave goodbye the moment you are accepted.

This gap was extremely apparent in my case. At the University of Wisconsin-Madison, all students participate in a freshman orientation process known as SOAR, an acronym designed to excite in spite of the initials representing the dry words of student orientation, advising, and registration. During SOAR, students show up to campus during the summer in groups in order to select classes, become familiar with the campus, and meet students who will be in their first-year class. The first morning of SOAR was the definition of over-whelming. We were first shuffled into an auditorium with our parents to hear opening words from a dean and some of the campus counselors. Then, over the microphone we were told that we would be splitting up into groups to choose classes. "Look for a campus guide holding a sign above their head with the college you are interested in joining," the speaker said before putting down the microphone.

Oh sh*t, I thought to myself, I need to figure this out right now!? I immediately looked over at my mom in a panic. "What should I do?" I yelped, as students began shuffling to different corners of the auditorium. I was torn between the School of Business and College of Engineering but had thought I would have my entire freshman year to decide, or at the very least more than two minutes! My mom, appearing equally as concerned, looked around the room and said, "Well I know your dad is always talking about how there are lots of good paying engineering jobs in his industry." Although I had a stronger inclination towards business, I made an impulse decision to walk over to the engineering sign instead. When I arrived, I went straight up to the counselor holding the sign and asked him, "What if I don't know what I want to major in yet?" He chuckled and quickly said, "Don't worry, this is just to get you started. You can always change later." While he was technically right, the reality was that I had already begun to entrench myself in the engineering path.

The moment I arrived in the College of Engineering building, I was guided into a computer lab where engineering mentors sat us down in front of laptops. Their advice was only relevant for the engineering track, so we enrolled in classes that were tailored to one of the engineering majors. While this initially didn't seem like a big deal, I was already making it difficult to alter my path. In subsequent semesters, the cost of switching majors began to increase because engineering classes weren't applicable to different majors that had their own required courses I hadn't taken. I soon found myself suffering from the sunk cost fallacy (I'll explain more about what this means later). On top of this, it was also difficult to switch to a business major due to my GPA. The average GPA in engineering was much lower than the average GPA in business, an objective fact my university didn't take into consideration on applications for majors outside of engineering.

For the first two years of my college experience, I suffered through difficult and personally unappealing classes in pursuit of a degree in either electrical or nuclear engineering. I was determined not to switch majors even though there was a clear disconnect between what I wanted to do with my life and the major I was pursuing. It wasn't until the summer before my junior year that reality hit.

How Nuclear Power Helped Me Decide My Major

East Granby, CT, July 2014

I stumbled out the side door of the warehouse and immediately ripped my gas mask off. I felt the sun hit my face as I coughed to clear my throat. I was on my third straight hour of running flame tests in our testing facility. This required me to take a long reel of thick rubber cable, roll it out onto the production floor, and then use a giant cable cutter to break off seven-foot pieces. I then lugged the cable pieces over to a metal ladder and used wire to secure the cable to the ladder. Once this was done, I dragged the ladder into a closed flame chamber. The room was dark and the walls were charred black from past tests. Once the ladder was centered over the flame rods, I turned on the gas and started my watch. Every five minutes, I tossed on my gas mask and walked into the room with a tape measure to mark how much the rubber jacket on the cable had melted. These cables would be used to power the coolant valves in nuclear power plants, which meant they had to continue to be operational even in the case of a fire at the plant. If the coolant valves failed, there would be nothing to cool off the reactors and a nuclear meltdown would be imminent.

When I got back to my apartment later that afternoon, I tossed my keys on the kitchen table and walked into the bathroom. I picked up a tissue, blew my nose hard, and stared down at the thick black mucus that filled the tissue. "That's it, I'm done with this sh*t" I grumbled as I tossed the tissue paper into the trash can and turned the light off.

Later that weekend I picked up my laptop and plopped down onto my couch. I had been more restless than normal that entire weekend. At the beginning of the summer, it had felt great to land an internship at my dad's company. But now I was feeling anxious as I realized there was no way I could do this for the rest of my life. I glanced at the table to my right and saw the two books I was currently reading stacked on top of each other, *Freakonomics* and an introduction to Java programming. All summer, I had been spending the majority of my free time either reading up on pop economics or trying to learn how to program. I slowly nodded my head as I began to formulate a plan. I opened up a new tab and began pounding the keys on my laptop. I needed advice from someone I could trust, and I knew just the person. Dan Olszewski, one of my favorite professors at UW-Madison. If there was anyone I could trust for advice on the topic of majors, it was him.

Alexander Valaitis
Sun 7/27/2014 1:27 PM
Daniel Olszewski

🖒 ↩ ↩ → ⋯

Hello Dan,

It's Alex Valaitis & I was in your General Business 311 class last semester. First off, I hope you are enjoying your summer so far. I've been interning out in Connecticut under Marmon LLC, a Berkshire Hathaway Company. As great as this summer has been so far, I have had a change of heart in terms of what I want to study in college. For the past 2 years I have been pursuing a degree in Electrical Engineering with hopes of obtaining a certificate in Entrepreneurship. Due to a number of different experiences over the past 2 years, I have come to decide that I am not truly passionate about Electrical Engineering. For instance, it was always a struggle to want to even get out of bed for some of my Engineering courses, yet I never felt more engaged than when I took your General Business 311 class. I accepted an Engineering Internship this summer to gauge how interested I truly was in Electrical Engineering. Despite having an overall good experience, I haven't felt like Electrical Engineering is my true calling. Meanwhile, I have read 5 books already this summer; 2 on economics, 1 on investing, and 2 on entrepreneurship. My girlfriend was the one that actually pointed this trend out to me, and questioned why I would always discuss these books with such passion but never talk about the Engineering projects I was working on. Then it finally hit me that I wasn't studying what I was passionate about.

The reason that I am emailing you in particular, is because I am planning on switching majors to Economics (w. Math Emphasis) & Computer Science. I remember that you told our class that you studied these exact 2 majors for your Undergrad. At this point all I am really looking for is some type of verification or advice from someone who has been through these programs before. As a Junior this fall I know I am going to have ground to make up. I have no Computer Science experience aside from some time spent on Code Academy. However, I have already completed 3 Math courses required for both majors, and received 8 credits for receiving 4's on my AP Macro & Microeconomics exams in High School. Please let me know what your opinion is on this late switch & if you think it would be feasible for me to complete in 2-3 years.

Sorry this email was so lengthy, I am just undergoing a very monumental change in a very short span of time. Any feedback will be greatly appreciated. Thank you.

—Alex Valaitis

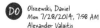

Re: Considering a late change in major(s)

○ ○ 🖒 [⇩ Reply all |∨]

Olszewski, Daniel
Mon 7/28/2014, 7:58 AM
Alexander Valaitis

Hi Alex,
Thank you for the kind words regarding GEN BUS 311 and I will be happy to provide advice as best I can. Your memory is good regarding my double major being Econ w/math and Comp Sci. In fact I also started off in the ECE program but after my freshman year an internship at IBM that summer decided that I should change my major so very similar to your situation.

My main advice is along the various points:
—Talk to some folks in advising in Letters and Sciences to get an idea of how much ground you have to make up since that might play into your decision making. I made the switch early but still went an extra semester due to the foreign language requirement.
—The Comp Sci degree opened a lot of doors for me on the job front including in the econ area since the demand was much stronger for those skills at the time. The major is a challenging one but no more so than ECE. There is also a Comp Sci certificate that might be worth exploring as well depending on your interest and time.
—I personally got a lot out of my Econ major and felt it provided me with a great understanding of business and current events. I still find most of my recreational reading is in the realm of economics.
—I would also take any of my advice with a grain of salt since my data points are from fairly long ago and I don't know all of the changes that have taken place in the major hence my key recommendation is to talk with an advisor.

Hope this is helpful,

Daniel Olszewski

By the time I replied to Dan the following Monday, I had already made up my mind. After swearing to myself that I would stick with my original major no matter what, I filled out the paperwork to switch to a computer science and economics double major. I was heading into my junior year, so the timing would be difficult but I just couldn't stick with my current path any longer. With some clever class scheduling and a lot of late nights in the library, there was a small chance I could graduate in just one extra semester.

I didn't know it yet, but I had just made one of the most consequential decisions of my entire college experience. The decision fundamentally altered the course of my life, and definitely for the better. While it was the right decision for me, I could have saved myself a great deal of pain and effort had I been given more guidance early in my college career. That's why I want to break down what I wish I had known about choosing a college major so that you don't make the same early mistakes I did.

Why Your College Major Matters

Before I proceed further, I want to discuss why your college major actually matters. Surprisingly, there are some people who don't believe your college major has much influence over the rest of your life. Most of the time, this narrative is driven by those in previous generations who subscribe to the belief that hard work is all that matters. What they may not realize is how much the job markets have changed. For new graduates, your major is a key screening factor that many companies use when considering which candidates warrant further consideration. This wasn't always the case, and perhaps it is part of what's been driving the disconnect between generations. Employers now have access to tools and services such as DegreeVerify[SM] by the National Student Clearinghouse[®], which can help ensure resume validity for academic credentials with minimum effort. There has also been an increased emphasis on skills proficiency, with new methods available to screen candidates for these skills remotely. In the past, your major may have been a footnote on your resume but today it is a forward-looking indicator of your employability and future success.

Companies care about your major for several reasons. For starters, it is a signaling mechanism that can be used to narrow a large field of competitive candidates. At LinkedIn, recruiters can receive more than 250 applications for a single opening. In order to distill to a reasonable number, they use specific criteria because there's not enough time to read every resume in depth. A college major is one of these screening criteria. If you have the major they are looking for, your resume moves to the next level of consideration. The second is that many jobs require increasingly greater technical or domain-specific knowledge and that knowledge is part of the curriculum of specific majors. If you don't have a certain major, the company assumes that you are missing requisite skills and knowledge for the job. As I just mentioned, new technologies have made it difficult, if not impossible to hide any skill gaps you have when applying to a job. The final reason is that college majors often open doors to certain clubs or other extracurricular activities. While I am a strong proponent of the notion that you can explore any area you want on the side, there may be certain clubs that won't be accessible to you in college due to your major. For instance, I was interested in investment banking in college but was unable to join the prestigious investment banking club at UW-Madison due to my major.

The traditional approach to selecting a college major has been to pick one of interest to you and hope that the pieces fall into place after graduation. While this may have worked to varying degrees for previous generations, the reality today is that your major is closely linked to career prospects. To ignore this reality is to make the same mistake as blindly enrolling in college even when you're not sure it's the right path.

What Are Your Options for Majors?

Assuming you agree that your college major is *really* important, the next logical question is: How do I choose a major? First, you need to be aware of the different options. Most universities offer a lengthy list of majors and even small colleges often offer 50 to 100 different majors. As no university offers every conceivable major, you should look at online sources in case there is a major you are interested in that is not offered at your current or target university.

One source is The Princeton Review, which lists over 320 majors at princetonreview.com/majors/all. As this list can be cumbersome to comb through, you can look at the categories of majors. For example, on collegemajors101.com majors are categorized into five distinct areas: medical and life sciences, visual and performance arts, liberal arts, engineering and technology, and business. You can then hone in on a specific category of majors and filter down from there. At collegemajors101.com, you can also dive deeply into descriptions of each major. For example, you can see the overall curriculum, which universities offer that major, and a list of employers who typically recruit people who study these majors.

There isn't necessarily one correct way to approach this process but I do suggest starting broad and then narrowing down. This will help you avoid unfortunate situations, such as finding out about a major after you've already spent time in one that's not right for you. By having a general awareness of every possible major, you can take solace in knowing that you are decreasing the chances of an interesting major passing under your radar.

How You Should Pick Your Major

The first thing to understand when you are choosing a major is that you want to find the right balance between **passion** and **practicality**. In this case, passion refers to any subject that you are strongly interested in. Or put into more tangible terms, if you were locked in a room for a few hours and required to learn about a subject, which would you choose? It's likely that there is more than one, at least that was the case for me, but starting with this simple question can help you eliminate many options. If you can't imagine studying something for a few hours, chances are you won't want to dedicate four or more years of your life learning about it.

While passion is important, you also need to dig deeper to find the right major. While some people may disagree, I firmly believe that it is vital to select a major that will lead to strong job prospects upon graduation. The truth is that not all majors are the same when it comes to landing a well-paying job after college, which can be a tough pill to swallow for some. This is where the practical aspect of your major comes into play. Almost all of us will need to find a job after college that pays well enough to not only survive but also, ideally, live the life we want. That is why it is so important to make sure that your major maps to realistic job prospects.

One way to do this is to select a specific major and re-search what the job prospects look like for that major. A quick hack is to go onto LinkedIn and type a university's name into the search bar. When you land on the university page you will see a tab that is titled 'Alumni'. On this tab you will see a section with filters on it for 'Where they live' and 'Where they work'. If you click the 'Next >' button at the top of the section, a filter for 'What they studied' will appear on the right. If you click on any of the majors in this list, it will filter the people cards beneath the boxes to show alumni that studied this major. Simply hover over any one of them to see their current role or add an additional filter on 'What they do' or 'Where they work' to get a more focused view.

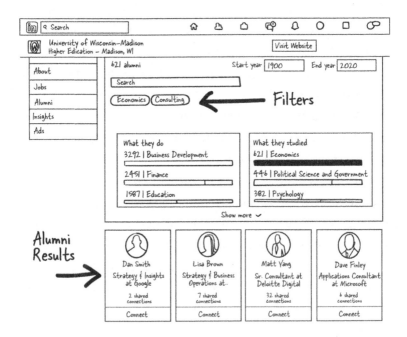

Another way to complete this process is by applying the reverse engineering approach I discussed in Part 1. By beginning with a specific job title, you can type a given role into the LinkedIn search bar and filter by people. Once you find a profile that intrigues you, you can check what that person studied in college before landing their current job. Again, the key here is to figure out the common career paths that people in a given major tend to gravitate towards. There are more rigorous steps you can take here, such as digging deeply into job market reports or reaching out to specific people who have pursued a given major to get their insights.

There is one other area I need to address, which is that you may choose to pursue graduate school after completing your undergraduate degree. In this case, you will need to take an extra step, which is ensuring that your undergraduate major will allow you to get into the graduate program that you are most interested in. However, that graduate program should ideally also map to strong career prospects, especially since it will require additional time and financial resources.

The Case for a Double Major

Up until now, I've discussed a college major in a strictly singular sense. I now want to make a case for why you should consider majoring in more than one subject.

Having spent a few years in the workforce already, I can tell you that jobs are rarely cookie-cutter when it comes to skill sets. In fact, just about every job will require a diverse mix of skills. It's important that you equip yourself to succeed by developing expertise in multiple fields and a wide variety of skills.

In my case, I double majored in computer science and economics, two fields that incorporate distinct areas of study and provide valuable knowledge and skills. Soon after I graduated, I wrote an article that explains my rationale for the value of a double major. You can find the full article at **TheModernCollege.com/doublemajor**. I will briefly describe my reasons here.

The first reason is that double majoring gives you more bang for your buck. While you will have to take more classes in aggregate, and almost certainly pay more in total, you should take advantage of the fact that most costs are fixed, such as base tuition, room and board, and fees. This means that the marginal cost of each additional class will be relatively low.

The second reason is that a double major will allow you to stand out in your field. A study by Burning Glass Technologies, a Boston-based company that analyzes job-market trends, found that if liberal arts graduates gain proficiency in one of eight technical skills, such as social media or data analysis, their prospects of landing entry-level jobs increase substantially.[24] While you may find yourself thinking you can do this on your own after college, you should take advantage of the incentive structure college can provide to make sure you actually learn an additional subject.

The last reason is that it will allow you to study different areas and discover new opportunities. While I think you should focus on success after college as your number one priority, it's also important to place exploration nearly as high. By staying intellectually curious, you may uncover passions you never knew you had or form innovative solutions in a field that you would have never considered.

When to Decide on Your Major

The last open question around the topic of college majors is deciding when to choose your major. There's no single standard but I suggest you consider a few principles.

The first principle is to focus on the breadth of your learning early on. Although I didn't follow this principle myself, I suggest erring on the side of exploration rather than speed. This will likely mean enrolling in a few courses that are interesting to you even if they don't fall within or even near the standard curriculum for your intended major. While it can be tempting to want to move quickly, you can miss some great opportunities by doing this. These opportunities may include forming new connections, uncovering passions, or absorbing tangential subject matter that is useful down the line.

This leads to my second principle, which is to hedge your bets as long as possible. Complete courses that meet your general education requirements, avoid major-specific courses as much as possible, and take intriguing electives during your first 2-3 semesters. If you know that numerous majors require a semester or two in a certain area, such as a foreign language course, then it might make sense to enroll in those classes early on since it won't be a waste of credits if you change majors.

The last principle is to ultimately decide with your gut and not just your head. It is easy to get overly caught up in what parents and advisers are saying, and just blindly follow their advice. Choosing your major is not the time for lazy thinking or reliance on the opinion of others. Instead, this decision requires deep introspection. Very few people make their college major decision with 100% certainty but by taking the time to explore different options, you will find that the decision eventually becomes clear. Or at the very least, it will be easier than trying to make a decision in a few minutes at your college orientation.

CHAPTER 6:

How You Learn

No matter what major you choose, you will have to study A LOT. How you use that time will be crucial in your learning, usefulness of what you learn, and enjoyment of the learning process.

One of the key differences between college and your K-12 education is that college offers much more flexibility in how you learn. From kindergarten through the end of high school, you were required to sit in a classroom for about six hours a day, much of which was spent listening to the teacher talk at you. While there is still some of this in college, you will have many more outlets for learning.

For instance, in some courses, attendance is not mandatory and the lectures are posted online. If you're someone like me, it may make more sense to spend some days in your residence hall or apartment learning at your own speed (and in your pajamas).

Furthermore, certain universities will provide opportunities to extend your learning via breakout sessions, labs, guest lecturers, and trips. I highly encourage you to take advantage of as many of these opportunities as possible. There has been a lot of research done around the different types of learners in the world. One popular model, referred to as the 'VARK modalities,' was created by Neil Fleming, who asserted that there are four primary communication modes used in learning: visual, aural, read/write and kinesthetic.[25] Depending on which is a stronger preference, a student may learn better with information depicted visually such as charts or graphs, information presented through lectures and discussion, written information, or examples and simulations. Though these are learning style preferences and certainly not the only way each person can learn, you may find it valuable to experiment with different forms of learning new information and skills throughout college. You will likely find that certain modes are more effective for you and enable you to maintain greater interest in your coursework. Engaging in different learning modes is also applicable to the world after college as many jobs require practicing different means of information consumption and dissemination than is found in a typical college classroom.

Grades Versus Learning

Another point I want to make about how you learn involves mindset. It's very easy to fall into the trap of thinking that grades directly equate to how much you are learning. Of course, this is not always the case. College is not different from K-12 in that grades alone can incentivize poor learning habits, such as memorizing instead of understanding and studying only for the sake of the grade. In his essay "Before the Startup,"[26] renowned investor and Y-Combinator founder

Paul Graham explained why many young founders struggled to build successful companies:

> We saw this happen so often that we made up a name for it: playing house. Eventually I realized why it was happening. The reason young founders go through the motions of starting a startup is because that's what they've been trained to do for their whole lives up to that point. Think about what you have to do to get into college, for example. Extracurricular activities, check. Even in college classes most of the work is as artificial as running laps.
>
> I'm not attacking the educational system for being this way. There will always be a certain amount of fakeness in the work you do when you're being taught something, and if you measure their performance it's inevitable that people will exploit the difference to the point where much of what you're measuring is artifacts of the fakeness.
>
> I confess I did it myself in college. I found that in a lot of classes there might only be 20 or 30 ideas that were the right shape to make good exam questions. The way I studied for exams in these classes was not (except incidentally) to master the material taught in the class, but to make a list of potential exam questions and work out the answers in advance. When I walked into the final, the main thing I'd be feeling was curiosity about which of my questions would turn up on the exam. It was like a game.
>
> -Paul Graham, *Before the Startup*

While Paul's advice is directed at current and potential startup founders, his message rings true on a more general level: real life is not something that can be gamed. After college, you will realize that the problems you face and tasks involved with your job do not come in a multiple choice format. In reality, the problems tend to be much more abstract and require a mix of critical and creative thinking. Rather than centering your attention on the grade, I found that a much better way to learn in college was from a point of curiosity. Don't try to learn something because you want to do well on an exam; instead, learn something because you're curious to explore a little bit more about how the world works. My belief is that when you take this approach, you will retain much more information over the long term and good grades will follow.

Mindset toward Learning

Most of my poor grades were from courses that I hated from the beginning. This feeling came from being forced to learn something for my degree program despite having zero interest in the topic. Chances are that you won't get excited about every course; however, you can take a mindset of curiosity towards each one. If you aren't initially interested in the subject material, try doing research to figure out if the material has any applications to the real world. For instance, if you are enrolled in a statistics course that is very dry and you are a sports fan, you can read about the power that analytics plays in professional sports leagues. The connection to something that is more interesting to you than statistical formulas may help you to be more positively inclined toward statistics. If this doesn't work to generate any interest towards a given course, another approach is to find someone in the class who is clearly passionate about it. Their energy will be infectious and they will likely be a good tutor.

To conclude, I'd like to riff off a quote by Ralph Waldo Emerson:

"Life is a journey, not a destination."

I think this mindset should be applied to how you learn in college. Learning is a journey, and it's important not to get fixated on a superficial destination, such as a letter grade.

The Importance of Office Hours

If I had to change one other thing about how I learned in college, it would be attending many more faculty office hours than I did. Office hours are time slots during which professors or teaching assistants are available to meet with individual or small groups of students. These time slots can be crucial for getting to know your professors on a more personal basis, obtain answers to your questions, and receive explanations that clarify lecture information and requirements for assignments. If you are enrolled in a university with a large student body as I was, office hours may be your only opportunity to get to know a professor. With class sizes that can sometimes be well over 100 students, many professors will simply view you as a student ID if you don't take the time to get to know them.

The time spent with professors can pay huge dividends. Though I didn't take advantage of the opportunities as much as I should have, during the times I did, they provided deeper insights on lecture topics and from their answers, I could often infer what would be on the exam. These meetings enabled me to learn the material much more thoroughly and earn higher grades. Professors are also just brilliant people in general and make great connections to call upon when you are in need of advice or a referral.

Ultimately, if you decide not to spend any of your time in offices with professors, then you will miss out on one of the most beneficial and unique aspects of college, which is access to highly educated people who are there to help you learn. Although the internet has made almost all information in the world freely available, it can't fully replicate the value of a face-to-face interaction with an expert in the field.

Learning through Clubs and Other Extracurriculars

This may seem counterintuitive but you will find you have more time in college outside of the classroom than you did growing up. Where many students go wrong is in prioritizing their time.

One aspect of college that you should absolutely prioritize in your schedule is clubs and extracurriculars. These are what I consider **learning by doing**. So much of the information you absorb in college will be theory-based, and it's important that you actually take the time to put what you learn into practice. Furthermore, extracurriculars are another strong sign of your ability to display for employers.

There are two types of extracurriculars that I would encourage you to explore. The first type includes ones that directly relate to what you are studying and hope to do professionally. In a sense, this type of extracurricular offers a way to practice and sharpen your skills in a low risk environment. The second type involves extracurriculars completely unrelated to what you are studying that offer opportunities to expand your horizons.

In my case, there were a few extracurriculars that had a huge impact on my life. While I will talk about several of these later on, I first want to focus on a club called Transcend, which focused on helping students explore the local business/tech startup community and work on projects of their own. I begin with Transcend since it was a perfect example of using a club to expand learning experiences in college.

I was a part of the founding team of Transcend and served many roles including treasurer, event planner, and vice president. To this day, I find myself applying the skills I learned and experiences I had while participating in Transcend. I was surrounded by smart and motivated people with many of the same interests I had, including the desire to build products and bring them to market. I was also exposed to hands-on experiences that directly shaped the career path I took.

As part of Transcend, I worked on multiple projects including an electronic waste recycling startup, two fitness projects, one mobile app, and a file collaboration startup. Over my college years, I became increasingly passionate about these projects and competed in innovation competitions on an international level in which our teams collectively won more than $21,000. I learned how to take ideas from sketches on paper to building teams and creating solutions that others would use and, in some cases, pay for.

All of this is to say that without joining Transcend, I would have missed out on a multitude of educational experiences that I would have never found by just sitting inside a library. There's a line that I like to say when students ask me for advice around college:

Your learning should begin at the edge of the classroom, not end there.

Make sure you spend some time finding extracurriculars that supplement what it is you are learning inside the classroom.

Transcending the Classroom

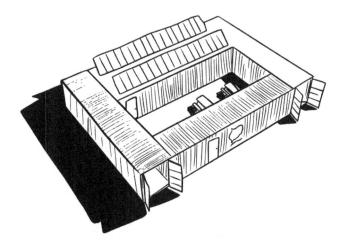

San Francisco, CA, March 2016

Bill Clinton's face looked five feet tall as it was being project-ed onto a giant screen on stage. Over 1,000 people looked on as a clip played of the former President commending all the teams for making it to the national finals for the Hult prize, an international social entrepreneurship competition. In just a few minutes, the international finalists from the United States region would be announced. This team would be one of five from around the world that would go on to New York City to compete for $1 million in funding to put towards building a social venture. The 2016 challenge was around the theme,

"Solving Problems for Crowded Urban Spaces." Our team had made it to the national finals in San Francisco for our project, "Metrecycle," which was a concept for solving the global electronic waste epidemic. As I sat in the auditorium next to my teammates, I couldn't help but reflect back on the months of build up to get us to this point.

It had all started a few months earlier when I was sitting in one of the computer science labs and struggling to finish a program. My friend, Josh Cherek, had just texted me that he had an "awesome new idea that could change the world." Josh was what many would consider a prodigy. In just three years, Josh completed a triple major in computer science, math, and physics, all while working to pay his own tuition and subsisting on a diet of mainly Ramen noodles. There wasn't anything Josh couldn't build, whether it was hardware or software. We had worked on a fitness tracking startup the year before and his skills had astounded me. So whenever he had an idea, I was down.

He showed up at the lab an hour later with a laptop in hand, looking flustered. When he saw me, he ran over and grabbed the closest chair. "Did you know that most of the computers in this lab will eventually end up either in a landfill or a village on the other side of the world?" He peered over his glasses to see my reaction. "That's pretty messed up," I said, still not totally tuned out of my computer program. "What can we do about it?"

Other students began shooting us dirty looks over their computers, but we didn't pay them any attention. Josh pulled his chair closer and I turned to listen more intently. "Well I've been thinking about it all week, and I think I have a solution." He pulled out a notebook with a bunch of scribbles in it. "What if there was a way to build cheap facilities where you could disassemble these electronics safely?" I looked more closely at the notebook and realized that I was looking at sketches of shipping containers. "You see, there's actually valuable precious metals and parts in most electronics. If you can get at them, this 'trash' can actually be turned into money." I turned to my computer and Googled "electronic waste." I looked in horror as the first images showed children sitting in fields of electronics and burning scrap. I paused for a moment and then pressed the power button on the computer. "Alright, I'm over this computer program. Let's go whiteboard for a bit. I have a key to the Internet of Things lab that we can have for ourselves."

It was 9 pm and we were starting to make progress. I walked away from the whiteboard filled with our diagrams. "If we are going to make this happen, we need someone who has experience with sustainability projects," I said to Josh. I picked up my phone and began dialing. My first call was to Luke van den Langenberg, a guy I had met in an innovation competition while he was working on a mobile app to cut down on wasted food on campus. My next call was to Jenny Sharpe. I had met Jenny in one of our student business incubators on campus while she was working on a sustainable food packaging company.

The four of us stayed in the lab until 2 am. By the time we left we had a concept for a project, and had made a decision to enter the Hult Prize competition. Essentially, we were going to retrofit shipping containers with the proper supplies and stations necessary to safely disable electronic waste. We would then ship these facilities to areas of the world that were drowning in E Waste, and then set up the proper supply chains for locals to safely sell valuable components and properly recycle the remaining waste. Within a few weeks, we had won the Midwest regional prize and a free trip to San Francisco. Metrecycle was legit.

As we sat there waiting for the results to be announced, I locked arms with my teammates. We had come so far in such a short time period. When the clip of Bill Clinton had finished, the CEO of the Hult Prize walked up to the mic. The crowd gave a round of applause and when they were done, he pulled out a notecard. "The winner of the National level round is…" I moved forward on my seat. "Musana Carts!" The crowd erupted into a cheer as we slumped down into our seats.

For the first hour after the announcement, I was inconsolable. I sat alone in one of the glass meeting rooms in the Hult Business School staring at the whiteboard. A few floors above, the rest of the teams were celebrating and networking over cocktails. I turned as I heard the door open, followed by Josh walking in to sit down next to me. "Hey man. I know you're super competitive and bummed we lost, but I'm still thankful we've gotten to work on this project together." I paused for a moment and stared down at the table. After a few moments, I looked back up at him. "You know what, you're right. We made it this far together and we can still try to solve this problem. For now, let's go celebrate with everyone else." We bumped fists and made our way towards the elevators.

My story with Metrecycle is the type of experience that, unfortunately, far too many college students miss out on. The knowledge you gain in the classroom is important, but if you don't put in the time and effort to apply that knowledge, you will not be equipped with the experiences you need to succeed in the real world.

It's also important to note that no one told us to work on Metrecycle. There was no assignment due at the end of the semester or letter grade we were trying to achieve. Everything we did was because of our own motivation and desire to make the world a better place.

In the end, while we didn't qualify for the $1 million prize and would end up shutting down the project later that year, I learned so much from the Metrecycle project. Whether it was forming teams, putting together business strategies or networking with people from around the world, I picked up lessons that I could have never gained in the classroom. When I applied to internships later that year, this project would be one of the things I always brought up in interviews. I had transcended my learning beyond the classroom, and I was better for it.

CHAPTER 7:

Who You Surround Yourself With

"You are the average of the five people you spend the most time with."

— Jim Rohn

College is an innately social experience. For those of you who are natural born extroverts, you may find that the social side of college comes easily. However, for others, this aspect of college may be the most challenging part (even more so than final exams). Regardless of whether you are an extrovert or introvert, I encourage you to embrace the social aspect of college. At no other point in your life will you be surrounded by so many people who are around your age and have many of the same goals and interests that you do. College is an awesome microcosm of the real world and offers an opportunity to practice skills, like communication and networking, which will be valuable for the rest of your life.

However, it's not enough to just be surrounded by people; rather, you must make sure that you surround yourself with the *right* people. In my opinion, the right people are those who will bring you closer to your goals of graduating and finding success after college. Whether you are on a campus of a few hundred or tens of thousands, this may seem like an easy proposition. But the reality is that there are many people in college who will pull you away from your goals.

In this chapter I will delve into the different social dynamics of college and present techniques for ensuring that you surround yourself with the right connections in a sea of college students.

Who You Live With

I really like the quote by Jim Rohn at the beginning of this chapter. I believe our brains and lives can be molded to a great degree during our college years. The things that mold your brain the most in college are what you learn and the people you spend the most time with. On this subject, I believe it's important to start with the individuals who will almost certainly be among those you spend the most time with, your roommates.

Some of you will be limited in how much control you have over who you live with your first year. You will likely be asked to complete a questionnaire that the university will use to match you with someone who shares your interests, habits, and personality, but these are not infallible. In my opinion, it's alright if the match doesn't work out because one bad roommate will not define your college experience and you can learn to adjust. However, when you are able to select your own roommates, I encourage you to put a lot of thought into who you choose to live with in college.

Habits have an inordinate effect on our success in life.

Charles Duhigg's book, *The Power of Habit*, is devoted to describing the importance of habits in our day-to-day lives. When we are forming habits, we are likely to be influenced by those around us. That is why you want to surround yourself with roommates who have positive life habits. If you live with someone who likes to go out and drink a lot on weeknights, you are more likely to go out and drink on weeknights. Similarly, if you live with someone who likes to sleep in every day, you will find it more difficult to wake up early and keep a healthy schedule. These are just a few examples of how living with a roommate who has bad habits can quickly rub off on you and affect your success in college.

On the flip side, if you surround yourself with people who demonstrate good habits, that will rub off on you, too, such as a roommate who keeps good hygiene and takes academics seriously. A good way to filter for roommates is to look for people with the same goals and principles as you. For example, if you are serious about becoming a speech pathologist, living with someone else who is also serious about becoming a speech pathologist can be a very wise decision. Alternatively, it is valuable to find diversity in who you surround yourself with. My advice is that in finding roommates, do not sacrifice quality in exchange for a more dynamic social experience.

It's also important to note that aside from the direct influence of your roommates, they will likely influence your wider network of friends. More often than not, your roommates will bring their friends around your living quarters, and their friends will likely be similar to them. As a result, you quickly get a multiplier effect on the influence your roommates have on your social life. No longer is it just one person rubbing off on you, but also their social circle. I personally had to learn this lesson the hard way. One of my roommates in college was unfortunately not a good influence. In order to keep him anonymous, I have chosen to use the pseudonym "Bill" and obfuscate certain details. While this story was difficult to recount, it includes important lessons about drug use and surrounding yourself with positive influences.

My Experience With a Difficult Roommate

Madison, WI, Dec 2014

"If he doesn't get pulled out of school soon, he's going to either end up dead, in jail, or getting us all expelled." My face was flushed as I talked to the small group of people in my apartment building's conference room. It was the second semester of my sophomore year and I was in a heated discussion with my roommate's dad and the building manager about my roommate's drug addiction. I no longer felt safe living in the same apartment as Bill, but I was having a difficult time convincing others of the extent of his addiction.

I never expected things to escalate to that level but, then

again, these things are always difficult to see coming. When I first decided to live with Bill, it had seemed like a good decision. On the surface, he appeared to have many of the traits you would want in a college roommate. He was smart, social, and enjoyed going to the local gym with me to play basketball. However, over the course of our time living together, I began to pick up on some concerning trends.

When he initially moved in, his habits seemed normal. Like many other college students, Bill would drink with the rest of us when we hosted parties at our apartment and he occasionally invited people over to smoke weed. Pop culture had taught me that these were normal habits for college students so I had no problem with him initially. However, as the semester wore on, it was clear that Bill's vices did not stop there.

I learned that there wasn't a drug that Bill wouldn't touch. He had a particularly strong addiction to painkillers and benzodiazepines, specifically Xanax. He claimed that they were prescribed by his doctor but I was skeptical since he would often take so many that he didn't leave his bedroom for an entire day. At first, I tried to ignore his addiction and rationalized it by telling myself that at least it wasn't hurting me directly. But then he began to bring other addicts into our apartment.

One weeknight in particular, I remember coming home after a difficult chemistry exam to find Bill and some of his friends (who didn't attend our university) snorting lines of cocaine and MDMA off of our kitchen counter. I immediately dropped off my backpack in my bedroom and walked over to my girlfriend's apartment to try to settle my anxiety. My grades were beginning to slip from the stress of my surroundings and the situation only seemed to be getting worse.

The final straw was when a friend of Bill's got caught by the apartment security cameras stealing packages from other tenants. He claimed it was to pay off a debt he owed to a drug dealer. When the police brought him in for questioning, we were called as witnesses as he was last seen leaving our apartment. After that event, I called my parents and they helped organize a meeting with the building manager and my roommate's dad.

When it became clear that his parents weren't going to pull him out of school, I began the process of applying for a new apartment lease. The day I was planning on submitting the application, I knocked on Bill's bedroom door to ask him something. I was met with silence on the other end. Later that night I received a text from his mom saying that they had pulled him out of school for an undisclosed health condition. I was officially safe to live in my apartment again.

There's a lot to unpack from my story of living with Bill, and even years after the fact, I still feel uncomfortable talking about it. One key learning lesson for me was the impact your peers can have on you in college. During the semester I lived with Bill, my GPA dropped by close to .8 points, and I struggled in many other areas of my life including organization, sleep, and exercise. Even though I wasn't taking drugs myself, his habits and the people he brought around the apartment negatively affected me via osmosis. There was an obvious turning point after Bill moved out and I was able to establish better life habits as a result.

The other key learning lesson was around the dangers of drug abuse. More than any other habit in college, drug use seems to be directly correlated to who you spend your time with. If you spend your time around people with access to illicit drugs, you will increase the chances that you get sucked into that world. While Bill was fortunate to have parents who forced him to drop out and escape with his life, I know that multiple of his friends lost their lives from drug addiction.

In my remaining semesters of college I would give much more consideration to who I lived with. This enabled me to build a network of close connections that helped form a positive environment around me. I encourage you to take the same approach as you go throughout your college years.

How You Network

Perhaps my biggest learning lesson since graduation is that *who* you know matters just as much as *what* you know. I underappreciated and didn't fully understand the importance of networking in college. For a long time, I thought the way to separate myself from the pack was to spend even more time in the library absorbing material. I want to reiterate what I've discussed earlier; it's crucial that academics don't get in the way of your ability to network. There's a sign hanging up in one of the most iconic bars on my alma mater's campus called "The Kollege Klub" that was written by Mark Twain:

Don't Let Schooling Interfere with your Education.

The first thing to realize about networking is that it should occur wherever you are. Whether you are in a classroom, in the gym, or picking up food from the cafeteria, there are always opportunities to meet new people. College provides much common ground between you and everyone around you, so it's easy to connect with others. As with anything, networking is something that takes practice. The more you do it, the easier and more natural it will become.

Another reason it's important to network everywhere is because you want to find people from a diverse set of backgrounds and with different experiences and opinions than yours. One of the aspects of college that has been under scrutiny is that campuses are too often echo chambers of the same ideas and opinions. If you only surround yourself with like-minded people who share your beliefs and opinions, your existing views will be reinforced and alternative ideas will be ignored. I advise you to fight this echo chamber phenomenon by connecting with a variety of people and truly listening to them. You can maintain your core principles, such as only connecting with people who are driven and positive, without filtering out people due to appearance, major, life background, or political opinions.

There are many ways in which to connect with different types of people on a college campus. One way is by attending a diverse mix of on-campus and public events. While clubs can be a good opportunity to delve deeply into an area you are already interested in, they can also be a chance to try new things. Most clubs host open events that offer opportunities to connect with members and nonmembers in a new space without the commitment of actually joining the club. Another way is to connect with the local community through cultural events, community volunteer opportunities, and apps such as Meetup that will enable you to discover different events in the community based on your interests.

Strong versus Weak Ties

Depth versus breadth is another important aspect of building a strong network. Generally speaking, you want depth in friendships from a handful of extremely close friends or "strong ties" in college. These are the friends that you spend a disproportionate amount of time with and the ones you can go to in times of need. To add breadth, you should aim to have 5–10 additional friends that you like but spend less time with. For even greater breadth, you want to have as many fringe acquaintances or "weak ties" as possible. These are people with whom you would feel comfortable having coffee with but may only talk to a few times a year. Weak ties should vary greatly in background, age, major, and other characteristics.

In a 1973 conceptual paper titled "The Strength of Weak Ties,"[27] sociologist Mark Granovetter explained why weak ties are often an overlooked area of our lives, despite the massive value they provide. Most people tend to place much more emphasis on strong ties, which makes sense as we tend to spend the majority of our time with this small group of people and this time spent together forms an emotional bond and feeling of reciprocity. Also, strong ties are extremely valuable because they help form tight knit groups of people who have much in common. However, strong ties have limitations since they not only require a lot of time and effort to maintain but they also can be insular and prevent the wider breadth of information gained from interacting with other groups.

This is where weak ties come in. Weak ties act as the bridge between groups of people that are closely knit with each other but not with other groups. By leveraging the bridges formed by weak connections, information can be shared across tightly knit groups that otherwise would be contained to a small and insulated group of people. The best part of weak ties is that they don't require as much time or energy as strong ties to maintain, which means they provide a relatively inordinate amount of value to our networks.

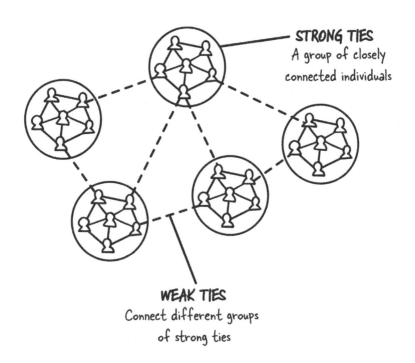

STRONG TIES
A group of closely
connected individuals

WEAK TIES
Connect different groups
of strong ties

In practice, the flow of information between tight knit groups of people can be meaningful in a number of ways. On a social level, it allows us to be exposed to different information and viewpoints that force us to activate System 2, or deliberative thinking, and to reflect critically on some of our closely held beliefs.

There are economic implications to weak ties as well. In his paper, Granovetter references a survey he conducted in a Boston suburb among professionals who had recently changed jobs. He asked the participants who found a new job through one of their contacts how often they saw the contact around the time they passed on the job information to them. Granovetter found that around 83.3% of the participants had found the job through a contact that they saw occasionally or rarely. This may seem counterintuitive since we reasonably assume that those we are most closely connected to are the ones most motivated to help us. Granovetter's findings show that the structure of social networks may matter more than the underlying motivations of the individuals within our networks.

I could go deeper into the technical research behind weak ties but the main point should be clear, weak ties are low cost but high impact connections in our life that should not be ignored. Try to form as many of these weak ties as possible while in college, and the results will be overwhelmingly positive. At the same time, don't ignore the importance of strong ties either. The best way to have a healthy balance of each type is to stay disciplined by evaluating your ties and using online tools to stay in touch. Social media is a great way in which to stay connected with a large group of people effectively and efficiently. It takes relatively little effort to like someone's post or shoot them a quick message, but oftentimes this is enough to maintain a weak tie. Later on, I will dive into techniques for building a strong online presence that will make it easier to build a large number of weak ties.

Strong ties are typically built naturally due to the emotional investment. However, if you ever feel your network is spreading too thin, it might be a good idea to audit your calendar and reflect on who you are spending the majority of your time with. If you find you aren't spending time with anyone on a consistent enough basis for a strong tie, it might be a good idea to establish some sort of ongoing meeting or event such as a book club or trivia night.

Clubs and Extracurriculars—Part 2

When I talked about clubs in the previous section, I primarily focused on the function of clubs for learning. However, the other important facet to clubs involves the people you meet. What makes the connections you make in clubs unique is that they are likely to be the people you will interact with the most after college. In other words, they are breeding grounds for continued strong ties.

Clubs are a great filter for meaningful connections, sometimes more so than your college major or who you live with. Clubs are often geared towards applications of your knowledge and skills outside of the classroom or, more specifically, the field you want to work in. Furthermore, many clubs have an inherently professional nature to them, even if professionalism is not obvious in the club's name.

An important extracurricular I participated in during college was a fraternity. The "Greek System" has come under considerable scrutiny and criticism over the past few years, and rightly so. On different campuses around the US, fraternities and sororities have unfortunately been at the forefront of drinking, sexual assault, and hazing scandals. Many have even been closed down because of criminal conduct by members. That being said, I gained valuable learning lessons from being in a fraternity.

The first was around how organizations function and how to deal with the internal politics that are present in any large group setting. It's not a surprise that many public policy makers were once members of college fraternities and sororities given the leadership skills that overlap in a Greek organization and in an elected governmental position. Another benefit was that it forced me to get to know more than 100 young men that I most likely would not have otherwise met. As a student attending an in-state university with many others from my high school, it would have been very easy for me to stay within the confines of my existing social network. By joining a fraternity, I was forced to leave my comfort zone and meet people from all over the country. Many of the members in my fraternity joined because they came from far away and knew few others. Whether from far away or just down the road, we all benefited from the many connections we made among the members.

The connections I made in my fraternity have had an extremely strong influence over my life, even to this day. As I will share later, I landed one of my first internships because I was able to make a connection with an employee who knew one of my fraternity brothers. Furthermore, when I moved to California, some of the first people I connected with were those I had met in my fraternity, including my roommate for my first few years in San Francisco.

Just to be clear, I'm not suggesting that every person

should join a fraternity or sorority in college. However, I do think you should consider a social or professionally-oriented club at some point. Not only will you be able to grow your skill sets but you will strengthen your network in the field that you pursue upon graduation.

CHAPTER 8:

What You Do

"The path to success is to take massive, determined actions."
— Tony Robbins

As important as the previous content is, this chapter is arguably the most important part of this entire book. Everyone who attends college will learn a lot of new information and meet many new people; these are givens when attending college. However, it's the actions you take which will define the true extent of your success.

Getting Good Enough Grades

Wow, just "good enough" grades? You must be thinking that doesn't sound very compelling. What you must realize, though, is that in this case, "good enough" can be an extremely wide range. I'm going to let you in on a secret, I graduated college with only a ~**2.9 GPA**, and yet I still landed an important role at one of the top tech companies in Silicon Valley. For my career track, this GPA was "good enough." However, for some of my friends currently in medical school or investment banking, this GPA would have ended their career before it even began.

When you enter college, and for each subsequent year, I want you to do the following exercise. Take out a sheet of paper and write down the following line *"For me, success this year looks like the following..."* I then want you to list the 2–3 things that absolutely must happen in order for you to consider this year successful. One of these line items should be the minimum required GPA you need to stay clearly on track with your goals.

If you're not sure what the minimum required GPA is for you to be successful, make sure to do your homework. Visit your campus counselor and ask them what the GPA requirement is for the major you are interested in pursuing. If you're considering graduate school, then you might be able to find the GPA requirement clearly listed online. If your interest is in a professional field, you can look at a few online applications and see what companies have listed on their job postings. When I say "minimum" required GPA for success, what I mean is that you should find the floor (i.e., what you need to even be considered) and then add some level of padding to ensure success. While some programs or companies may not explicitly list a GPA requirement, they may still use it as a means of ranking applicants. Use your discretion when defining this target, and also consider what makes you comfortable.

It might be tempting to just shoot for a 4.0 every quarter, but there is a downside to blindly picking a target like this. For any career path, a GPA is only one facet of what is needed to succeed. Oftentimes, you need a mix of a strong GPA, clubs and extracurriculars, a strong network, and internships. If you anchor your success solely on GPA, then it will be difficult to justify spending any time outside the library. As a result, you may actually be shooting yourself in the foot professionally, not to mention you will probably miss out on some fun and unique experiences.

Staying Out of Trouble

I've seen far too many talented and motivated individuals throw away their entire futures because of one moment of indiscretion. It's possible to get everything else in college right but ruin it all with a single serious mistake. There are different dimensions to staying out of trouble in college, and you will be frequently confronted with the need to make decisions that put you into or steer you clear of bad situations.

For previous generations, poor behavior was most often kept private. With the internet and ubiquity of smartphones and other devices, every one of your actions may become part of a permanent record and put under a microscope. Contrary to popular belief, college students often make the right decisions. However, there are a few areas of the college experience in which there has been a trend of poor decision-making. I have already touched upon the dangers of drug use and how I watched it derail some very talented people. Another area that tends to be fraught with peril is around alcohol consumption.

If you begin college immediately after high school, you will be under the legal drinking age for much of your time in college. In spite of the legal issues, you and your friends will likely drink during your college years. I'm not condoning underage drinking, I simply recognize that it happens and will give advice accordingly. First, I want you to recognize that **the moment you take a sip of alcohol, you are giving up your ability to completely control your situation**. Let me repeat that statement again. All it takes is one sip of alcohol and your ability to control your situation is gone. For starters, the moment you take a sip of alcohol as an underage student, you've already broken the law. This leaves you open to discipline from legal authorities and your university. In fact, your university does not require the same burden of evidence that law enforcement does. Your university may even begin actions to remove you from school just on the suggestion that you have been drinking underage. There are even more serious consequences for hosting other underage drinkers. At Wisconsin, it was common for the campus police to bust a house or apartment hosting a party with underage drinkers as an example to others. The rule on campus was that when a house hosted a party, the owners would have to pay the tickets for all of the underage drinkers. I was aware of fines as large as $20,000!

Another focal point of potential trouble in college involves sexual relations. For some of you, this may be a non-factor while in school due to a decision to stay celibate or because you establish a committed relationship early on. Even without alcohol, if you are exploring sexual relations with multiple partners, my advice is to follow three simple rules; always ask for explicit consent, uphold a sense of privacy about the encounter, and don't expose your partner to any situations that may diminish their health. The common theme across these three rules is respect and maturity.

When alcohol is part of the equation, your ability to control the situation and exercise good judgment may be diminished, you are less likely to remember these three rules, and may even find yourself in an unfortunate sexually-related situation as a result. In more serious cases, you may even find yourself accused of sexual assault, the recipient of a sexually transmitted disease, or center of unwanted attention when the encounter is distributed electronically to others.

To conclude my advice about alcohol, I want to emphasize that the decisions you make will not always be easy. Like many universities, there was a strong drinking culture on my campus, which meant I was constantly forced to make decisions around drinking. Luckily, I escaped from college unscathed but this isn't the case for all college students. The best way to avoid serious consequences from alcohol is to take some practical steps in advance. In general, try to only drink with people you trust, practice moderation, and if you find yourself or someone else in a bad situation, call someone for help. Many colleges have a medical amnesty clause that prevents students from getting into serious trouble if you call in help for someone in need.

Outside of sex, drugs, and alcohol, there is a host of other things that can get you in trouble. My general advice for steering clear of trouble in college is to look at things over a long-term horizon. College is just the start of your life, and it's easy to get caught up in the moment and feel that the present is all that matters. Keeping a long-term perspective while in college will help you to make decisions with your future in mind.

"What were you serving, milk and cookies?"

Madison, WI, September 2015

The summer after my junior year, I turned 21 and was offi-cially at the legal drinking age. After my 21st birthday, it felt like a massive weight had been lifted off of my shoulders. When I drank now, it would be legal so my days of worrying about getting in trouble were behind me. Or so I thought. For most of college, one thing I never really understood was what the term "liability" meant. Then I hosted a party at the beginning of my senior year and I soon became very familiar with the term.

The night had started off great. One of my roommates was training to get his bartending license and had printed out a menu with custom drinks on it. We had invited 10-15 people over, most of whom were also of legal drinking age. But as college parties tend to go, our friends invited their friends and quickly the numbers ballooned. Not all of these second-de-gree connections were of legal age and we didn't even know some of them at all.

By 11 pm, things were starting to get a little bit crazy. We had over 30 people in our apartment, and it was becoming difficult to make my way around. Sensing trouble brewing, at one point I jumped on top of my couch and cut the music. "Alright, listen up everyone!" I was trying to yell over the other conversations in the room. "At midnight, we're shutting this thing down and heading to bars. So, get your drinks in now while you still can." I jumped off the couch and headed over to my roommate who was still mixing drinks in our kitchen. As he was making another drink for me, I heard a hard knock on the door. I slid past a few people and made my way to the door. When I opened it, there were three girls standing there who I didn't recognize. One of them looked pretty intoxicated but at that point, I was too distracted to give it much thought. This was college, people drink, and in under an hour everyone would be out of my hair.

For the next 15 minutes everything seemed normal. I laughed with my friends, took some selfies, and sipped my drink. It was shaping up to be a great event. And then I decided to go to the bathroom. When I walked in, the first thing I noticed was the puke that was sitting in my previously clean white sink. I shook my head in disgust and turned to walk out and wash my hands in the kitchen. The puke was tomorrow's problem. Before I could get over to my roommate to tell him what happened, I heard another knock on the door. "That's it," I said to myself, "no one else is getting in here." When I swung open the door, I saw two girls I didn't know.

"Hey, do you know who lives here?" they asked. I nodded my head and responded, "Yeah, that would be me." They looked at each other concerned and then pointed to their right. "I think there is somebody getting sick in your hall-way." Again, my heart dropped, like the time I'd seen that security footage sophomore year. I stepped out of my doorway and looked down the hall where a girl was lying motionless on the ground. "Oh God," I whispered as I jogged over and knelt next to her. She was in a puddle of her own puke and she had a thousand-yard stare. I now knew who the bathroom scene had come from. As I looked closer at her face, I realized that she was the one who had shown up looking intoxicated. Within moments, I heard my apartment door open and her friends came running out. I shot them a concerned look as they walked over. "Your friend is in really bad condition," I said to them. They looked at me with fear in their eyes. "Yeah, she drank way too much back at our apartment," one of the girls said to me. "We can carry her back and watch after her." They bent down to try to grab her. "No you're not," I said back to them sternly. I pulled my phone out of my pocket, my hand trembling as I began to dial the numbers, 9, 1, 1. "Wait please don't call!" one of them shouted at me. "She's not 21 yet, she'll get an underage drinking ticket." I looked back coldly, "I don't care. I'm not letting you ruin her life because you don't want to get in trouble." I walked down the hallway, and pressed call.

Within minutes, paramedics were in my hallway rolling a stretcher and lifting her onto it as she sobbed. Moments later, the police were at the door collecting my information. After everyone had left, they wrote me up a noise complaint ticket for $300. "Consider this a warning, you guys. Don't worry, we don't tell the university about these tickets, so you won't be in any other trouble. But never again host underage students."

One week later, I was nervously rubbing my hands on my

pants as I waited outside the Dean's office. Apparently, I had been given incorrect information because the university received word of my party from campus police. When it was my turn to enter, I saw a grey-haired man with spectacles looking back at me. "So I heard you hosted a party with underage drinkers?" he said sternly. I shifted in my seat. "What were you serving, milk and cookies?" I shook my head and looked down at the floor. "Do you know that we can expel you for that type of action?" My heart rate soared as I began to panic. "Can I call my parents?" I blurted out. The Dean laughed and shook his head. "Of course you can't, you're an adult now, mommy and daddy can't get you out of this one."

For the next hour, I gave the details of the event and got berated for hosting a party. I explained how I hadn't invited the guest and that she had been at my house for less than 10 minutes before she got sick. Luckily, she had met with the Dean the day before and corroborated my story, so I was let off with a warning.

As I walked out of the Dean's office and back onto campus, I let out a long exhale. I had dodged a major bullet that I had never seen coming. Until I walked across the stage for graduation in December of the following year, I would not allow myself to be in that situation ever again. I had managed to stay out of serious trouble, but just barely.

Even though this story doesn't paint me in the best light, I wanted to tell it because it is a stark reminder of how everything can change in an instant. My entire college career and life were almost destroyed because I was careless about who I allowed into my apartment. It didn't matter that I hadn't personally given the girl any drinks, I was still liable as a host. On an even more serious note, the girl almost lost her life because she didn't limit her alcohol intake that night.

Counselors place a lot of attention on coursework and making sure you perform well inside the classroom. However, when students have their college experience derailed, it is usually because of something occurring outside the classroom. You can bounce back from a failed exam or two. However, sometimes you can't bounce back from one moment of indiscretion.

Taking Care of Yourself

College will take a toll on you in more ways than one. There is the mental aspect of coping with a new environment while also taking in large amounts of information. Another is the physical aspects of defining your daily schedule, eating healthy, and making time for exercise. Yet another is the spiritual side of defining what drives you every day and gives you a sense of purpose. These areas are the most important aspects of your college experience and, yet, they are usually the first ones to lose priority when times get tough.

I encourage you to make sure that these areas of your life remain at the forefront while you are in college. I've spent a lot of time emphasizing that the purpose of college is to find a career that enables you to achieve the lifestyle you want. However, this shouldn't come at the expense of your health and happiness while in college. I will take a deep dive into each of the key areas of your life and share some tips for how you can maintain each one throughout your college years.

Mental Health

Success in college starts with your mental health. In order to operate at your maximum potential, your head needs to be in a good space. Many college students suffer from a variety of mental health conditions including anxiety, stress, and depression. The good news is there are proactive steps you can take to improve your mental wellbeing while in college. Most universities offer mental health services by campus psychologists or other types of mental health specialists and referral to off-campus services when needed.

The biggest obstacle for most students is putting their egos aside and seeking help in the first place. This is the reason I personally didn't pursue these services in college. I preferred to pretend that I had everything in order. I've learned to take a different approach to mental health since graduating. After moving out to San Francisco, I met a number of successful individuals who preached to me the importance of investing in your mental health. This motivated me to start seeing a behavioral psychologist, despite not having a pressing reason. I simply wanted to improve my mental headspace. The reality is that you don't have to already be suffering with a serious mental health issue in order to seek support. In fact, it's actually much easier to engage when everything is going well. And if you are suffering from a serious mental illness, it's even more crucial that you seek the help you need early in your college career.

The other challenge in dealing with your mental health in college is finding the time to do it. What many students don't realize is that the biggest time suck of all is not being in the right headspace. If you are anxious, distracted, or depressed,

141

it will take you longer to do the same tasks than if you were in a good headspace. This is how many college students get themselves into a vicious cycle. By not devoting time to your mental health, you will perform well below your potential, which will likely add to your stress levels and put you in an even worse position. Perhaps the most obvious example is when students choose to skimp on sleep in order to "get more done" and then can't concentrate because they're tired all of the time. In general, optimize for your happiness and mental health first and most things will naturally follow from a productivity standpoint.

Physical Health

Along with mental health, the other thing that tends to go out the window when students arrive at college is their physical health. It's so common that there is even a saying for it, "The Freshman 10," which refers to the average amount of weight that a student gains during their first year. This is unfortunate, because as with your mental health, not focusing on your physical health can bring down all aspects of your life.

The key is finding a way to form positive physical health habits in an environment that is very different from your schedule and surroundings in high school. For instance, in high school I competed on our soccer team, which forced me to exercise for at least 1.5 hours each day. Furthermore, I rarely had to worry about how to feed myself since my mom cooked breakfast and dinner, and my high school provided lunch. This isn't the case in college. Unless you are a student athlete, there will be no system in place to ensure that you take the time to exercise on a regular basis or follow a healthy diet.

There are many techniques you can pick up to ensure solid physical health. The most powerful one is using social pressure as a motivation. Each year, you should arrange to meet a gym partner or several partners who will hold you accountable to working out together. Intramural sports are another great way to ensure getting physical exercise.

In terms of eating healthy, this can be more challenging unless you are on the university's meal program as most of these offer a large selection of options for each meal. For those not on a meal plan, it can be tempting to buy cheap but unhealthy foods. My suggestion is that you set aside time to shop and do meal prep from recipes you found online or sent to you by your family and friends.

Lastly, as I mentioned in the mental health section, getting the proper amount of uninterrupted sleep is an important aspect of staying physically well. There have been many studies that show a lack of sleep can hurt many areas of your life, including your metabolism and eating habits. Though some people will brag about how little sleep they need, the research shows that carving out at least eight hours of sleep every night is vital for long term success.

Spirituality

Spirituality can mean different things for different people. For the purposes of this section, I am using spirituality to describe your personal motivations and purpose for being in college each day. Without a solid foundation upon which your motivations are based, it will be very easy for your college experience and life to feel meaningless.

There isn't one right way in which to strengthen your

spirituality. Some people connect with their spirituality via religion, others through service to others, and still others through their hobbies. Whatever it is you choose to connect with, it's important that you define a bigger purpose upon which to motivate yourself.

This is where personal exploration can once again be helpful. Take the time to try out different activities and reflect on which ones leave you feeling the most fulfilled. Also, don't be afraid to ask yourself "why" in regards to anything you do. Just because you defined a strong why when you started college, it doesn't mean the why won't change over time. Constantly reflecting inwards will help you recognize when important things are changing in you. As Socrates would say, "The unexamined life is not worth living." Or as I like to say, "The unexamined college life is not worth experiencing."

Making Time to Reflect and Smell the Roses

As I said at the beginning of this section, it is difficult to sum up all of the important aspects of college in a few chapters. However, I do believe that the areas I have covered will give you more than a solid foundation upon which to find success during your time in college. While I don't want to lose track of the theme of pursuing a goal-based college experience, it's also necessary to note just how important it is to live in the present. There is truly no time like your college years and if you spend too much time thinking about the future, you will miss out on the beauty of this unique time in your life.

There is also a paradox here that is important to note. While each one of the areas I have described may seem easy to accomplish on its own, when you put them all together, it becomes quite challenging. You will experience a constant balancing act and you may feel at times that you are robbing Peter (schoolwork) to pay Paul (enjoying life). That is why despite the fact you can say that each one of these is straightforward when analyzed in a vacuum, the statement that "college is simple" is far from true. It's easy to overlook this, though, and when we try to boil success during college into easily digestible concepts, such as GPA, relationships, or even happiness, we often come to a conclusion that doesn't match our actual state.

Defining success in college is truly multi-dimensional and I encourage you to constantly analyze all of these dimensions while not being consumed by them. If you are able to keep these nine different aspects of your life in balance while still enjoying yourself in college, then I would say it's almost impossible not to find success while in college.

PART 3:
Land Your Dream Job

*"Good morning, look at the valedictorian
scared of the future while I hop in the DeLorean."*

— Kanye West, *Good Morning*

I am going to continue hammering home the key theme of this book in the remaining chapters:

Approach college so that you can land a job that pays you enough to live the life you want

This to me is how you should define success and is at the heart of Modern College. I started by first helping you decide whether or not college was even the right decision for you. If it isn't the right decision, I've suggested other options to pursue that can bring you success. If college is the right decision, I've provided advice to help build confidence in your decision, knowing it is best for you and not just because someone told you to do it.

I then focused on the college experience and described the nine key factors behind finding success in college. I intentionally glossed over the long tail of other topics that you may find in other books and blogs because they don't all apply to everyone and are less important in the bigger picture. If you want to delve deeply into these aspects of college, I highly encourage you to check out the additional resources I have posted online.

If you follow everything else up until this point, then you will be in a good position to find success after college. However, as with any endeavor, it's important that you finish strong. The purpose of this final section is to help you do just that by offering the tools and advice you need to step out into the real world, ready to own your future, rather than moving back into your parents' basement and questioning your decisions.

CHAPTER 9:

Building Your Professional Network and Brand

It turns out that "who you know > what you know" extends into life after college, and in many ways becomes even more important in the real world. While the mindset stays the same, the techniques for how to network vary slightly. But to begin with, I want to build on some of the previous advice I gave and uncover why professional networking is so important.

Forming a Foundation for Your Network

In a recent piece by LinkedIn's head of social impact, Meg Garlinghouse stated that "more than 70% of professionals get hired at companies where they already have a connection."[28] Furthermore, LinkedIn company data suggests that "On LinkedIn, applicants who are referred to a job by a current employee are nine times more likely to get hired."[29]

These are pretty startling statistics when you think about it. What they demonstrate is that it is much more difficult to land a job at a company without having a personal connection to someone already working there. There are two ways to react to this information. The first is to dismiss it and do things on your own. The second is to accept it and act accordingly. I believe it is much better to opt for the second option. If you accept the power of professional networks, you will then devote time and attention to improving yours. It is valuable to remember that most of us want to work with people we like. The first step in being liked is making sure those in professional positions know you.

A necessary precursor to professional networking is having some sort of foundation upon which to network. There are a few different aspects to forming a professional foundation. The first is a **resume**. This is your basic way of showcasing your skills and credentials. Your resume should take many different forms, ranging from a physical piece of paper to an online profile, such as with LinkedIn. In some cases you may also be asked for a **CV** or **cover letter** as well, but I have opted to focus my advice on the resume since this is the most common document for college students.

Another piece of your foundation is your **personal narrative**. While similar to a resume, it should be less dry and follow more of a story arc. It can include details such as where you grew up, why you selected your major, and where your passions lie. Think of this as a way to start small talk with someone you just met. You can begin by jotting down some bullet points and practice by talking it through on your own. Eventually, this should become embedded in your memory so that you can speak through it without notes. The last part is your **mission or goal**, which may have a professional and/or lifestyle twist. Being able to tell someone, "I want to become a product manager at a large tech company," makes your intent clear for someone who may be able to lend assistance. Similar to your personal narrative, you should spend time reflecting on your mission, writing it out, and practicing it so that you can express it effortlessly to someone else. Your foundation will enable you to network professionally and to interview effectively. (Later, I will discuss how to turn your personal narrative and goal into a talk track.) Let me explain to you what I mean.

Imagine you find yourself at a coffee shop and you realize that a very powerful person is next to you; for the purposes of this example, let's just say the person is Jeff Bezos. He tells you that he will introduce you to anyone you want, fund any project you have, or land you a job at any company you choose if you can convince him you deserve it in five minutes. Without a strong foundation, you would blow an unprecedented opportunity by stammering and trying to think on your feet. He'd lose interest as he realized you weren't someone in a good position to be helped by him. At that point, he'd finish his coffee and have security take him away to his private chopper.

Though this is an extreme example, the principle remains the same. As people become more professionally successful and have more work and personal pulls on their attention, their time becomes more valuable and they become less inclined to waste it. In my experience, someone who seeks my help needs to demonstrate first, they truly want it and second, I can make a difference in their success.

The last thing I want to note is that your professional foundation will likely fluctuate over time as your situation changes. When it does, you will have to update your resume, personal narrative, mission and goals. The key is to be prepared when opportunities arise for conversations with other professionals.

Creating a Strong Resume and LinkedIn Profile

Your resume is your way of demonstrating your experience and qualifications to the professional community. Your online profile, such as on LinkedIn, is the digital extension of your resume and allows you to reach as many members of the global workforce as possible. With new tools allowing recruiters to reach candidates in all corners of the globe, there has never been more competition for top tier jobs. If you want to stand out, having a strong resume and online profile is vital.

As a college student, it can often feel difficult, if not downright impossible, to put together a quality resume since you obviously have less professional experience than much of the workforce. That being said, there are techniques you can employ to bolster your resume.

Resume Tips

Have a Clean Professional Format

Most recruiters will look at tens, if not hundreds of resumes in a single week. As a result, they will weed out candidates as quickly as possible. One way to find yourself immediately in the "no" pile is to have a resume that lacks a professional aesthetic.

In general, you should use a clean font (for example, Arial or Times New Roman) and size 11 or 12 font so the text is clearly legible. You should use one of the widely recognized formats available on the internet that include clear sections for your name and contact information, resume summary, professional experiences, education, projects, skills, and awards or other recognitions. Also, proofread it carefully for spelling, grammar, and punctuation to make sure that such errors do not detract from the information you are trying to convey.

It can also be helpful to apply a template to help guide you. Microsoft offers a resume builder tool in Word, and I've found some great free templates at Novoresume.com. I've also included resume examples at **TheModernCollege.com/resume**.

Emphasize Your Strengths

For many college students, especially underclassmen, your work experience will not be the strongest section of your resume. Instead, you should tailor your resume so that it highlights other strengths, such as clubs and other extracurriculars. If you held leadership positions, you should highlight these and the skills you gained in these organizations. If the job you are applying for involves specific skills, you should emphasize these on your resume.

If you are fortunate enough to have some professional experiences under your belt, use this to your advantage. Lead with your work experience, as a respected company on your resume is a much better signal than almost anything else you can put on it.

Lastly, use your own judgement on what to add or omit. For instance, I don't recommend putting your GPA on your resume unless it's at least within the top 20% for your major or if you graduated with honors. Since I had below a 3.0, I never listed my GPA on my resume. This allowed me to land internships and job offers for roles in which I didn't even meet the "requirement" to interview. I'm not advocating that you ever put false info on your resume, but strategic omissions can be just as important as inclusions. You can also speak to an omission in more detail if you are pressed on it, however if you control the narrative in an interview that likely won't even happen.

Highlight Results

As I mentioned before, recruiters constantly work to separate the best candidates from the others. One thing you can do to help them is by highlighting tangible results.

A good rule of thumb for whether something is worthy to include is to consider whether you can tie a metric to it. Numbers are crucial on resumes because they jump off the page and make it easier for recruiters to mentally quantify their impact. For example, "I drove a 15% increase in mobile app downloads for a top 100 app in the fitness category" sounds much more impressive than saying something generic like "I led digital marketing for a local fitness startup."

You can even do this for student organizations if you haven't completed an internship yet. Demonstrating an ability to measure and perform against a metric for anything you do is an important skill for any job out there.

Be Concise

The last and possibly most important resume tip is to be concise. There is no reason for a college student to have a resume longer than one page, and some would argue you should never exceed one page regardless of where you are in your career. This may sound easy but the reality is that many students struggle to summarize their experience succinctly.

As you look through each section, keep each to 2-3 lines at most, including your professional experiences. Devote the limited space available to your most high impact projects and quantifiable results, and then cut the rest.

While I was at Intuit I helped with a few cycles of recruiting and I can tell you that I only ever remembered 1-2 things tops on any given resume. That is why it is crucial that the most important aspects of your resume are written concisely and stand out from the rest of your resume.

LinkedIn Profile Tips

It would be really difficult (not to mention environmentally detrimental) to try to print out hundreds of copies of your resume and hand them out. Luckily for us, a group of individuals saw the ability to solve professional networking at scale and founded LinkedIn in 2002. Now with 660+ million members in over 200 countries,[30] LinkedIn is a must-have for any current or prospective professional. I would say this even if I was not currently employed by LinkedIn.

A LinkedIn profile can serve many purposes, including building your professional brand, marketing your products or services, and of course, landing a job. Given the importance of your LinkedIn profile, I am dedicating a section to helping you make the highest quality profile possible.

Use Professional Photos

While this may seem obvious, a surprising amount of job seekers get this part of their profile wrong. Your profile picture and background are the first impression a recruiter or visitor will have of you. Make sure you look professional and friendly.

In general, you should avoid using profile photos that have busy backgrounds, bad lighting, shows you in a group setting, or just isn't you at all.

Your background photo can also be an opportunity to catch someone's eye. Choosing a professional photo that is related to your field or speaks to you as an individual can help. For free professional photos, check out pexels.com

Write a Compelling Headline

After your profile photo, the second most important aspect of your profile is your headline. This headline can include things such as your current internship/job, former internship/job, your interests, your passions, or your dream job.

A compelling headline will make it obvious to any recruiter what your current professional status is and why they should be interested in you. It is also crucial that you use words in your headline that map to specific roles or companies. These words will help LinkedIn/search engines categorize and surface your profile in search results, and also help recruiters using profile scraping tools find your profile.

Include Work Experience

When it comes to your work experience, my advice is very similar to formatting your work experience on your resume. You should describe your work experience in a format that is both concise but thorough. A good way to do this is to stick to three bullet points per role and highlight any deliverables or quantifiable impact you had.

One other key tip for LinkedIn profiles is to make sure that you use the typeahead functionality when adding a work experience. In simple terms, this means selecting the company Page from the dropdown when adding a work experience. By doing this, the official company logo will be listed on your profile and your profile will be properly mapped in the LinkedIn system to that company. This will help add legitimacy to your profile and improve your chances of being found. If you don't use the typeahead, the company will be displayed as a default icon and you will lose out on the benefits that come from being properly mapped.

Display Your Education

If you are currently a student or a recent graduate, make sure that you input all of your education information including your degree, relevant courses, affiliations, awards, and GPA if you feel it's a strength.

Similar to the work experience section, for LinkedIn profiles it is important to use the typeahead when selecting your education. Most education institutions have Pages on LinkedIn and by using the typeahead, the official logo will appear on your profile and your profile will show up in the Alumni tab.

Add Connections

The last aspect of a strong profile is making sure you have a decent number of connections. If your connection count is less than 100, then there is a higher likelihood that people may confuse it for a fake profile.

Start by connecting with people you know well and once you have a critical mass, start reaching out to connect with people you know less well or not at all. If you don't know someone personally, it's also important to add a short note explaining why you want to connect.

LinkedIn does a great job of surfacing potential connections as well. In the 'My Network' tab, there are carousels of recommended connections. The more accurate information you put on the rest of your profile, the better the recommendations will be in this tab.

How to Network

Professional networking takes two primary forms, **physical** and **digital**. Because college campuses are filled with a lot more students than professionals, you will need to lean into digital networking more than physical networking while in college.

For physical networking, you must first get yourself around the people you want to network with. Once again, your goals will be crucial in helping you define who these people are in the professional world. One way is to belong to a professionally-oriented club that brings alumni to campus to speak and mingle with students. Another way is through public meet up events that I already discussed. These are often filled with people who are already working professionals and can make for great weak ties who can send professional opportunities your way in the future.

Once you are in the same room with these individuals, the next step is to find a way to stand out by initiating conversations. If you are not comfortable striking up conversations with strangers, I recommend taking the time to role play with your friends. Remember to fall back on your foundation to initiate and drive these conversations. As soon as the conversation gets rolling, you should try to find some sort of connection. Whether it's the same major, hobby, or something else, if you can find common ground, it will be much easier for you to connect.

As for digital networking, I think there is much more potential for college students than they usually realize. With online professional networking tools like LinkedIn, it has become much easier to find professionals to connect with for advice and, potentially, a future referral to their company.

In order to have success with digital networking, it's important to have a strong online presence. While I was in college, I invested in a few key areas of "digital real-estate" in order to grow my professional brand. The first was building a personal website (you can check mine out at alexvalaitis. com). The cost of picking out your own domain is reasonable and with website creation tools, such as Wix or SquareSpace, you don't need sophisticated technical skills to create a basic landing page. The other area I invested heavily in was online content. I began by creating a profile on the popular blogging platform Medium. By publishing pieces on areas of interest to me, I began to be seen as a "thought leader" in these spaces. This ended up flipping the paradigm, so that I actually had professionals reaching out to me while I was still in college.

It can feel intimidating putting your thoughts out there for everyone to read but I found that it became much easier the more I did it. My advice is to begin by selecting a topic about which you have learned a lot and feel comfortable writing or speaking on. This will ensure that you produce solid content and diminish some of the pressure you may be feeling on your first few pieces. It is also easier to produce multiple pieces if you focus on one topic and build off your previous content in a series-like format. Once you have a draft ready, I highly encourage you to hit the publish button and not overthink it or procrastinate with small edits. By getting your content out into the world, it will allow you to get immediate feedback from your audience and prevent you from procrastinating on edits. Worst case scenario, if later on you decide that you really don't like a piece of content you published, you can always hit delete.

Tapping Into Your Network

As with any endeavor in your life, building a network takes a lot of time and energy. The good news about a professional network is that it tends to pay you back exponentially in the long run. However, I do have a few words of caution for students who begin tapping into the networks they've built.

To begin with, you should drop any sort of entitlement you may have towards networking. At the end of the day, no one owes you anything. You should never feel any sort of animosity if someone doesn't respond to your call or email. Most people lead busy lives and more often than not, if someone doesn't respond to you, it's because they have something more pressing to attend to.

It's also important to make sure that you aren't just taking from your network. Internet personality and social media guru, Gary Vee, has an approach to networking that he refers to as "give, give, give, then ask." The basic idea is that you should always seek to give to those in your network before you begin asking for things in return. As a college student, you might not feel that you have much to offer but trust me, you do. While I was in college, I would frequently reach out to different professionals in my community and offer to buy them coffee in exchange for 30 minutes of their time. After the meetings, I would make sure to refer any talented friends I had to their company.

In summary, both your professional brand and network can be powerful tools but only if you invest the proper time and energy into them. A well-curated professional brand will make it easier to network, so remember to get your foundation established first. And when you do find yourself with a strong network, be sure to not only take but give back as well.

CHAPTER 10:
Pursuing Professional Opportunities

Blizzards, Computer Programs, and Career Fairs

Madison, WI, February 2015

It was a freezing Tuesday night in the middle of Wisconsin. Blizzard warnings were all over the television and there had been advisories from the news channels to stay indoors. I was on the University of Wisconsin-Madison campus, leading a spring kickoff event for the Transcend club in one of the engineering buildings. At the time, I was still a vice president and had an obligation to fulfill. However, I really couldn't enjoy my time at the event because I was stressing out. I was now a junior, my classes had become more challenging, and I was juggling a heavy course load since switching to a computer science and economics double major that year. To make matters worse, I still had zero leads for an internship during the summer before my senior year.

I continued to glance up at the clock every few minutes as the event wound down. There were only 45 minutes left in the career fair being held on the other side of campus and I was still shaking hands with new members. As the last of the students shuffled out and I helped clean up the pizza boxes, I had a decision to make. Did I go home and work on my computer program that was due at midnight, or did I try to sprint across campus and attend the career fair for the final few minutes? It felt like freshman year orientation all over again and I was worried that I was going to make another mistake. This time, I followed my gut and decided to run to the other side of campus. As I was leaving the engineering building, I slipped on ice and landed in a pile of snow. I winced as I felt a jolt of pain in my tailbone, followed by an icy feeling along my back. My dress slacks and shirt were soaking wet, but my adrenaline was pumping too hard to care. I slowly picked myself up and began jogging down Dayton Street towards the Kohl Center. With each breath of cold air, my nostrils constricted and I could feel the mucus begin to drain into my throat. But

I was determined to make it, and after a few blocks my body began to warm up until I was even beginning to work up a light sweat under my jacket.

By the time I made it to the entrance of the Kohl Center, some of the recruiters were already taking down their stands. I took a quick look at the pamphlet they had passed out at the entrance and quickly found the company I wanted to talk to the most, Dell. Their booth was located right around the corner. I took a minute to compose myself and then walked up to a gentleman standing at the booth. Here's how the conversation played out:

Me: "Hi, my name is Alex."
we shake hands
Blake: "Hey. Blake. How's it going?"
Me: "Good. Pretty busy night but excited to be here. [blah, blah, blah] I was hoping to learn more about internship opportunities that Dell offers."
Blake: "Yeah sure. [blah, blah, blah] The program is 12 weeks. [blah, blah, blah]."
Me: "Oh that sounds really cool."
Blake: "Yeah it definitely is."
awkward pause

I wasn't sure if it was because of the mile-long jog I had just taken through the blizzard or that my mind was on my computer program, but for some reason I just wasn't finding a way to connect. Slowly beginning to accept defeat, I shook his hand again and went to the table to pick up a pamphlet. As I was about to turn and leave, I thought of something.

Me: "Hey, random question. But do you know a guy named Brian Stapleton?"

Blake: "Wait no way, you know Brian? He was one of my good friends when he interned at Dell with me in Texas. How do you know him?"

I smiled and proceeded to tell him about how I knew Brian from my fraternity. Brian had been a good friend and mentor to me over the years, and I had remembered him mentioning he had interned at Dell over drinks one time in my apartment. Suddenly the conversation took a 180-degree turn. I had found a connection.

Blake: "Here, write your email down on this piece of paper. I'll make sure you get an interview with my VP. I'll be sure to put in a good word for you."

I quickly scribbled my name on a piece of paper and thanked Blake for the connection. This time when I turned to leave the building, I did so with a smile on my face. I may have been freezing cold, soaking wet, and doomed to fail my computer program, but I had an interview at Dell because of networking and at the end of the day, that's all that really mattered.

Career Fairs

My story paints a rather rosy picture of career fairs but the reality is that they don't always go that smoothly. In fact, a better analogy for a career fair is that it's like a speed dating event, only it's your career at stake instead. With their long lines and numerous booths, career fairs can be intimidating to even the most confident and well-prepared college student. However, you can't write them off because they are the best source of in-person networking available to you while in college.

Because career fairs are so important, you need to make sure you plan ahead. This means having the dates on your calendar weeks in advance, preparing the necessary materials to bring, and doing research on the companies you want to talk to. More than anything, I believe that career fairs are all about **focus**. You want to narrow your search down to 3–4 companies and plan your schedule around them. Ensure that you set aside enough time at the career fair to have a sufficiently long conversation with the recruiter at each of these booths. Here are a few other tips to help guide you through an on-campus career fair.

- Show up with your resume completed and, optionally, with business cards that include your full name and contact information.
- Have your list of 3–4 companies you are most interested in. Prioritize visiting these booths first. If possible, modify your resume to each company and if an application was available in advance, bring a completed copy with you.
- Prioritize the career fair over all other activities so that you arrive when it is least busy. Avoiding peak hours is key for having good conversations with recruiters.
- Before approaching a booth, walk slowly past it to catch the names of recruiters. If you spot a first name, type that name and the company into an internet search bar to find their online profiles. Use the information to form a connection, such as the same major or hometown.

- When approaching the booth, have a talk track ready. Hand them your resume, tell a concise story, and guide the conversation to the outcome you want—an interview for an internship or job.
- If you form a connection, act upon it by confirming an interview slot, sharing social media contact information, or taking their business card and following up with an email as soon as you get back to your place.
- If a talk doesn't go well, don't get discouraged. Try visiting the booth later to talk to someone else. The recruiters are constantly busy so odds are the person you first talked with won't realize you returned to talk to a different recruiter.

It is important to be aware that career fairs are a very specific type of networking. They are fast-paced and high intensity environments that tend to favor outgoing personalities. If you aren't naturally well-suited to this kind of environment, think of career fairs as an opportunity to improve your skills over time. That is why I highly encourage students to start attending career fairs as early as their first year of college, even if you have no idea of what you want to do after graduation. Becoming comfortable in the career fair setting will help you perform well when you need to later on.

Online Applications

According to a recruiting report by the company Jobvite, close to 50% of job hires worldwide in 2018 came from either an online career site or job board.[31] Online job seeking is no longer a medium that can be ignored, least of all by college students and early career professionals.

Unlike career fairs, online applications are a totally different beast. Despite leading to decent hiring numbers in aggregate, online applications can be a bit of a black hole for most applicants. For starters, they are relatively low friction, which means a lot more people will apply via online portals than through in-person recruiting. Another factor is that it can sometimes be difficult to represent your skills in an online format. For instance, I always felt that some of my strongest skills, such as interpersonal communication, didn't shine through in a generic online application format.

However, just because online applications are less of a sure thing, does not mean you should ignore them completely. Sometimes the companies will not make a trip to your campus, so an online application may be your only shot.

The first step is finding the online application and submission dates. Your university career services office may have tools such as the Handshake app to surface different internships and full time job opportunities. Be sure to sign up for this app and any other job boards that your university offers. If your university doesn't offer these types of apps, or you aren't pleased with the job results, you have other discovery options at your disposal. One way is to simply Google: *Insert Company* + *Insert Role* + "Application" and see what comes up. If you are able to find an online application, make sure you put a sufficient amount of time and effort into customizing your resume and making sure that your application is high quality. Most large companies do their undergraduate recruiting at the beginning of fall and a second smaller recruiting batch at the beginning of spring. It's important to try to track these dates down and apply online as soon as possible.

Hiring Effectiveness by Channel

.39 .83 **4.66** **19.35**

Job Boards   Career Sites   Employee Referral   Hiring Manager Referral

Source: Jobvite

Once you have applied online, you can try to improve your chances by reaching out to an employee of the company on LinkedIn. This second method can have additional benefits, as a direct referral can often land you in a preferred stack of online applications. For instance, at LinkedIn, employees have custom referral links that we can send out that are separate from the public application. These custom referral links get prioritized and have an employee's reputation tied to them, which increases the chances of you landing an interview. Just how much can it increase your chances?

In the same report from Jobvite, researchers found that despite the fact that online applications led to a large volume of job hires overall, they are actually much less effective on average than a direct referral from an employee or hiring manager. The report included a hiring effectiveness score, which was calculated by dividing the hire % over the application %. Online jobs boards and career sites had hiring effectiveness scores of .39 and .83 respectively. Meanwhile, employee referrals and hiring manager referrals had hiring effectiveness scores of 4.66 and 19.35 respectively. In other words, the odds are much more in your favor if you can find a way to get directly referred to the role versus just cold applying online.

In summary, online applications should just be another tool to incorporate into your job seeking plans. It's best not to rely solely on online applications given that the success rate per application is relatively low, but don't ignore them completely as they do lead to interviews for some candidates. They can also offer a good discovery path for roles you didn't even know existed.

Recruiter Outreach Advice From a Tesla Recruiter

While I have some experience with campus recruiting, my full-time role has never been in recruiting. For this reason, I wanted to bring in someone much closer to the recruiting process to provide insights on the best way to reach out to recruiters. Anastasia Ecin is a recruiter at Tesla, the innovative automotive and renewable energy company headed by the renowned Elon Musk. At Tesla, Anastasia is a recruiter on the internship programs team. During a video call with her, Anastasia revealed that recruiters can receive as many as "50-100 LinkedIn messages per day."

With this much competition, it can be hard to stand out. However, with the right approach, you can greatly improve your chances. The following are Anastasia's top three tips for reaching out to recruiters, in her own words.

Do Your Homework

Before reaching out to a specific recruiter, do intensive re-search on the company's career portal. These portals have dedicated pages describing the different programs they offer for students and new grads. Within these program pages, you will find information on teams, qualifications, events, loca-tions, and benefits of the program. From here you can find all of the open roles that recruiters are actively hiring for and begin to hone in on the 1-2 that most interest you.

As a recruiter, it can be frustrating when students reach out with questions that are common knowledge. As a general rule of thumb, if it's something that you can find on Google, don't ask a recruiter. This is true at every stage of the job search process but is especially true with recruiter outreach as we have such a high volume of requests, we can only address the best leads.

Send a Clear and Actionable Message

When you have completed your homework and are ready to reach out to a recruiter, it's important that your message is clear and actionable. Of all the messages I get each day, about 75% of them are missing one of these two crucial traits.

The primary reason to message a recruiter is in regards to a very specific role that the recruiter is hiring for. Any other type of question or outreach is best targeted at other employ-ees of the company, who will have less inbound messages to sift through.

Inquiring about a specific role makes the message clear. In order to make the message actionable, it is important to make sure that the message is targeted at the right recruiter so they don't have to forward it on to someone else.

Provide All Necessary Information

The best messages I receive on LinkedIn are the ones that don't require me to send a follow-up message. If you highlight a specific role and it's one that's under my purview, then I am more likely to act on it.

Always include your resume in a PDF format and not as a Word document when messaging a recruiter. If you include the resume in the initial outreach, then the recruiter can begin screening you on the spot.

When screening resumes, I look for keywords that match the job description I am hiring for. This is why it is so crucial to do your homework ahead of time and tailor your resume accordingly.

CHAPTER 11:

Landing Professional Opportunities

The First Internship

When it comes to building your resume, the hardest part is getting that first line item. Almost every job opening expects some type of experience, either required or preferred. However, this creates a catch 22 as almost every new graduate has little or no prior professional experience. One way to handle this expectation is to gain relevant experience through internships.

As I discussed earlier, my first internship was in an engineering role at my dad's company. I took it because it would be an opportunity to gain experience and have a well-known company on my resume. What I learned was even more important because I quickly recognized what I didn't want to do. Had I not taken that internship, I might have made the mistake of earning a degree in something I had no interest in pursuing after graduation. The internship also led me to shift to disciplines I was truly passionate about. One of my projects during the internship was writing a piece of software to process quotes for customers. It was during this project that

I discovered my deep interest in software, which motivated me to pursue a degree in computer science. The last and most tangible result was that I now had experience under my belt. When I went to the career fair my junior year, I immediately stood out because I had a prominent company on my resume, while many of my peers had a blank space.

I recognize that not everyone will have an internship opportunity fall in their lap and I am forever grateful for my dad and his employer for allowing me to intern there. However, there are some general principles to take from my experience. The first is that you should never say no to a professional opportunity during your first few years of college. Any meeting, interview, or offer you get is a positive step in the right direction. Your early professional years should be about building your resume and experimenting in different roles. A second principle is to set your expectations low. You're not going to land your dream job right away, especially without any experience. Instead, look at each role as a stepping stone to a better one. Finally, don't be afraid to pursue positions you feel unqualified for. It's easy to get caught up in "impostor syndrome" early on in college. Many students hold a belief that they aren't the right person for the role they want and that the company could find someone better or more experienced. However, you need to take this fear head on and recognize that you are more qualified for most internships than you think. Every successful professional started somewhere, what will your start be?

The Interview

Every internship and job you land will involve an interview. Your connections, resume, and cover letter may get you through the door but once in the room, you have to make a good impression in the interview. I encourage you to follow a few basic steps in preparing for each interview.

Step 1: Do Your Homework on the Position and Organization

Having now spent time on the other side of the table as an interviewer, one of my biggest pet peeves is when a candidate makes it clear they haven't done their homework for the interview. Contrary to popular belief, interviewing is not just about showing up and performing well on the spot. Instead, the level of success you can expect to have during an interview is decided by the amount of research and critical thinking you do in the time leading up to the interview.

At a minimum, you need to have a solid understanding of the company, the roles of the individuals who will be interviewing you, and the position you are interviewing for. Interviews aren't meant to be orientations. The expectation is that you already took the time to research those aspects; otherwise, why take the interview in the first place?

As an inexperienced college student, this is where you can stand apart from other interviewees. While you may not have as many credentials, you can make up for this by showing up prepared and demonstrating intellectual curiosity coupled with an ability to work hard.

If you aren't sure where to start with your homework

about the company, a few obvious places to hit up are Google, Glassdoor and LinkedIn. A few simple Google searches can usually land you on a company website or other helpful links. These resources can help tell you what the company is about and if they operate in a space you are interested in.

Once you find out details about the company, you should examine the most important aspect of the company, which is the people that work there. At a minimum, you should search the profiles of those who will be interviewing you ahead of time. This information will help you figure out talking points and ways to connect with them. If you landed the interview through a recruiter, you should ask this person for the names of the interviewers.

Step 2: Practice Your Talk Track

Earlier, I discussed the purpose of a professional talk track for networking. I mentioned that this talk track can be somewhat flexible, depending on the situation, but ultimately it should tell a story that aligns you to your goals.

In the case of a job interview, it should be molded to the position you are interviewing for. An extremely common interview question across all roles is: "Why are you interested in this position?" The following was my talk track when I interviewed with Intuit and was asked this question.

Interview Question: *What made you want to pursue a role in product management at Intuit?*

My response: *To answer that question, I actually have to rewind to my first summer after my sophomore year of college. At the time I was studying nuclear engineering and a bit unsure of what I wanted to be when I grew up. I wanted to explore dif-*

ferent paths, so I took an internship as an engineer testing wire and cable for coolant valves in nuclear power plants. Not exactly a role like a tech PM, right?

However, I learned some valuable lessons during that role. For instance, I coded a script to process quotes for one of our subsidiary companies. It was during that project that I recognized the power of software and realized I wanted to work in that space. This motivated me to switch majors to computer science and economics going into my junior year.

After the change in majors, I jumped headfirst into software projects. I built teams to launch 2–3 web/mobile projects on campus and even landed a role as a software developer at Dell. My time at Dell was great because I learned how to operate in a fast-paced tech company environment. However, things still didn't quite feel right. While I liked working on software projects, I realized I found more excitement in working between functions and focusing on the product and users. I moonlighted as a PM as a side project at Dell and was offered a chance to return the following summer to Dell as a PM intern.

All of that has led me to this interview. I now know I want to work in tech and that I'm extremely passionate about product. I also know that Silicon Valley is still the best place in the world to start as a PM in tech, and would love to do that at Intuit.

Do you see how I molded my talk track to fit my narrative for the interview? I obviously didn't take my first few internships because I wanted to be a tech product manager. I didn't even know what a product manager was at the time. However, I was still able to string together those experiences to create a story arc that demonstrated that my journey to that interview was very purposeful.

Narratives like this one take time to develop and deliver well. You need to write them out and then practice speaking them so they sound natural. You should mold your narrative to fit the situation. Make sure your narrative shows introspection about events that fit your current job pursuit.

Step 3: Preparing Yourself Mentally and Physically

The last thing you need to do is show up, not just literally but also physically ready and mentally focused to give your best performance. In college, I always struggled to sleep before interviews. I was a nervous wreck and always felt that I could have done more to prepare. The truth is, there are limited returns on interview preparation because you don't want to be so prepared that your responses sound canned.

It's important to keep in mind that people don't hire resumes or scripted answers, they hire people they like and connect with. Therefore, the interview should feel genuine and even fun, and certainly not like a chore. You can take solace in the fact that sometimes an interview going wrong can be a good thing, as this kind of interview can provide valuable learning lessons and can be a sign that you need to consider a different role. I am generally solid at interviews but have butchered a few in my past. I don't worry about them because I wouldn't be in the place I am now if they had all gone well.

On interview day, make sure you wake up rested, dress appropriately, and feel composed. Bring a water bottle with you to the interview as it will keep you hydrated and can occasionally be used as a prop in between answers to buy you some time to think. When you answer a question, make sure you make good eye contact and break down your thought process so that even if you give a wrong answer, the interviewer can at least appreciate how you approach problems. With enough practice, this will begin to feel natural.

Interviews are an opportunity, not a guarantee. However, if you take the right steps, you will eventually nail an interview and land in a role at a place you want to be after college.

The Career Momentum Effect

Let's imagine that you have been taking the right steps in college to find professional success. You may have a solid internship or two under your belt. You've gone to career fairs, landed some interviews, and received at least one job offer.

If you are fortunate enough to reach this point, you will experience what I refer to as the "career momentum effect" because every positive experience will open up more doors and each of these doors open up new opportunities. The career momentum effect eases the pressure in job searches. You may find that you have so much to offer a company that the interview tables can actually flip and you may find yourself interviewing companies instead of the other way around.

I was able to create this situation in my final semester of college, although it took some work. When I entered my final semester, I was in an interesting situation. On the one hand, I had an impressive resume for a college student because I had already completed three internships at big name companies, was earning my degree in "hot" majors, and had recently won numerous startup competitions. On the other hand, I had a few things working against me. My pursuit of difficult subject areas and decision to expedite a double major had led me to a

GPA that was below a 3.0, my second summer internship ended on a sour note after my manager blocked my return offer when she found out I was working on a side project outside of work, and it seemed unlikely that I would receive a job offer from the company.

It took me a few weeks to process my frustration with what I felt was an objectively unfair result that had been handed down to me, but I knew I couldn't make excuses. Sometimes in life, there are certain things out of your control. What I did have in my control was the ability to build my own momentum and focus on the positive aspects I had going for me.

I knew the first thing I had to do was get my confidence back, I hit the career fairs hard and worked at landing as many interviews as I could. I looked at these initial interviews as mainly practice but I was also intent on landing an offer as soon as possible. My first offer came in the form of a sales role at Oracle in Austin. While it wasn't my first choice, I still took the interview because if I didn't land any other offers, I would have absolutely taken the Oracle offer.

After that first offer, I felt a huge weight lifted off my shoulders. I then began concentrating on product management positions because I realized this was what I really wanted to do, though I knew that a PM position was more difficult to obtain. I recognized that my best chance would be with Intuit since they were the only Silicon Valley company that actively recruited for PMs on campus. Recognizing this situation, I made sure to attend every on-campus networking event Intuit hosted and visited the career booth three separate times to make sure I had introduced myself to every single recruiter. In parallel, I also began sending messages on LinkedIn to product leaders at other tech companies. While this was largely an unfruitful effort, it did lead to an opportunity at IBM. Below is the message I sent to the head of the IBM Offering Manager (PM) program in Austin. As you will soon learn, that message eventually led to an interview and job offer from the company.

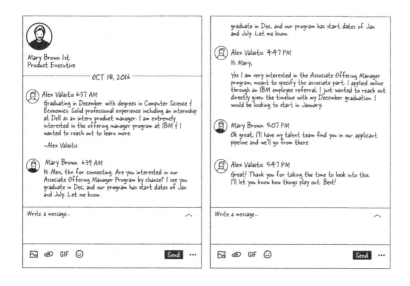

When it was all said and done, I had received four full-time offers from different companies despite beginning the semester with none. By leveraging my experience from previous internships and the professional networking toolkit I've laid out, I was able to take control of my own career.

I don't tell this story to come across as arrogant or suggest that landing a job is some process that can be gamed, but there are some key aspects I want you to take away from my experience. The first is the adage, never put all your eggs in one basket. Banking on a single job offer or company is a dangerous game to play and can leave you with no job. The second is to recognize the benefits that I have previously described about early professional experiences. Think of it as hitting a few singles during your first few years of college rather than waiting to hit a home run in your first at bat during your final year of school. The last is that you shouldn't avoid pursuing low hanging fruit. This means pursuing a job you are confident of getting and accepting a decent offer if you don't have any other viable options.

Making a Career Decision

Throughout this book, I have devoted a lot of time to analyzing the key decisions you will make during your college journey. I dove into the decisions on whether to attend college or pursue another path, the major you will study, the organizations you might join, and the people you surround yourself with. The next decision I want to discuss is what career to pursue after college, starting with your first job.

Before going further, I want to take a moment and commend you for making it this far. If my advice has helped you reach the point where this section has become relevant, it is reassuring that my effort in this book has been worthwhile. I also want you to recognize what an enormous privilege it is to have the opportunity of choice when it comes to professional opportunities. If you were born in another time or another place, there is a strong chance that you wouldn't even have the opportunity to make this decision right now. The good news is that you are born in an era and a country where many opportunities exist, so I want to make sure you make the most of them.

I am writing this section under the assumption that you have received at least one professional offer. If you haven't, don't worry, just focus on the previous sections and continue to push forward. If you have just one professional offer, then I would highly encourage you to take it and use it as a career starting point even if it wouldn't have been your first choice. After all, you will need to earn money in order to sustain yourself, even if you won't be financially independent.

For those of you with numerous job offers, you may be feeling a lot like you did before you entered college. Decisions become more difficult when there is more on the line and the opportunities are numerous. For this reason, it's important to be even more deliberate when you make a decision. In my opinion, you should rely on the following three factors.

Financial Outlook: Immediate Salary + Long Term Earning Potential

We all have to eat. That is just a fact of life. You need to land a job that allows you to make a survivable living, or even a very good living, and you should never feel embarrassed for allowing money to factor into your decisions. When it comes to earnings, you should consider the short term and the long term.

The short term is your immediate salary and benefits. If it won't enable you to afford the basics of housing, food, clothing, and some entertainment, you should strongly consider another path. However, you should also factor in the long term opportunities. In some cases, it may actually make sense to forego some good short term opportunities in order to reach a greater long term payout.

A classic example of this is the decision to pursue graduate school. Graduate school is rarely the best financial decision in the short term as you will get paid little or nothing and may have to expend money for tuition. Yet, it still may make sense to pursue this route if a graduate degree increases your long term earnings potential.

Optionality: Is There Wiggle Room in the Future?

Another aspect to weigh when considering an offer is whether it will pigeonhole you in a career path or, alternatively, offer opportunities for other positions or to enter into other industries in the future. Certain paths will provide less wiggle room than others. An example would be pursuing a path to be a surgeon. There is a huge cost and time commitment, and the skills you acquire aren't necessarily easily transferable to other functions or industries. On the flip side, a role in a large consulting firm can be a good hedge if you want to have more options in the future. The reason is that consulting enables you to work with several companies early on in your career, which provides both the knowledge and connections to hop to a different company later on. I have met many smart individuals who have chosen the consulting path out of college precisely for this reason.

Though not every job pays as well as in the tech and finance industries, it's important to note that jobs that pay extremely well can open up doors in the future because of the discretionary money you will have for other endeavors. In many areas of business, money equates to access so if you can acquire enough money, then your options will continually expand. For instance, many successful professionals in the tech industry invest in real estate or startup companies. In my case, I used my extra income to hire professionals who helped me create this book. If you land in a job that doesn't provide much discretionary income, it will be more difficult to branch out into different ventures. This isn't to say that every graduate should go running to jobs in tech or finance but, rather, to reassure those who do begin their careers in these sectors that their first job doesn't have to be the end game.

Another aspect of optionality is the time it takes to pursue a given opportunity. For many careers, an undergraduate degree is not sufficient and you will need to dedicate more years of your life to ongoing training or education. When you are young, your most valuable asset is your time. Before you give that time up, you must first make sure it is the right decision for you in the long term. If you don't think it is or have doubts, then you may want to consider an option that doesn't have the same time commitment or a route that will provide you with more options or capital in the future.

Happiness: Does Your Career Path Make It Easy or Difficult to Wake up Each Morning?

I have a confession to make. You know that whole 'land your dream job' line on the cover? It's not quite accurate. But if you're reading this right now, then it clearly worked. Why is that? It's because we are all drawn to the idea that there's some perfect job out there waiting for us, and if we just spend another late night studying or get another credential under our belt, then suddenly we will be able to reach out and grasp that job.

The reality is that life doesn't work this way, in part because there is no such thing as a perfect job. Absolutely *no*

189

one loves every aspect of their job, no matter how cool it may seem on the surface. Furthermore, even if you do find yourself in a great job, you might not feel the same way about it a few years down the line. So, if your goal isn't pursuing an imaginary dream job, what should it be instead?

Happiness. It's something many people aspire towards but few achieve. It is the holy grail, and yet so many of us make decisions throughout our lives that bring us further away from it. You are going to spend the majority of your life working and during those years, you will spend most of your hours each day in an office or similar constrained environment. Given this outlook, why would you not pursue a career that makes you happy?

How to Thrive in the Future of Work

As much as we all might like to believe we are in complete control of our careers, the reality is that the macro forces surrounding us have a much bigger impact than many of us realize. Economic forces, demographic forces, and technology forces are powerful and in a constant state of flux. What these forces look like today is different than how they will look in just a few years.

In order to succeed in the future of work, you need to have a high-level understanding of what the future might look like. While no one can predict the future with 100% accuracy, there are some fundamental shifts that have begun to emerge that are worth noting as you approach the beginning of your career.

Key Theme 1: Get to a City

Regardless of the professional path you choose, one of the best things you can do for your career is to move to a big city immediately after graduation. According to the McKinsey Global Institute's report, *The future of work in America*, 25 megacities will account for close to 60% of U.S. job growth through 2030. Alternatively, rural counties could see a decade of flat or even negative net job growth.[32] By moving to a big city, you will greatly improve your chances of capturing a part of the economic growth that will occur in the next several decades.

There's a reason that big cities capture such a large percentage of economic growth. Big cities are talent hubs where the brightest minds in the most influential industries come together to make great things happen. Scott Galloway offers a great analogy where he compares living in a big city to rallying in tennis. You only get good at tennis by rallying with people better than you. By living in a big city, you are constantly forced to rally with the best.[33]

The obvious downside to any big city is the cost of living. I currently live in San Francisco where the average rent for a one bedroom apartment is $3,446.[34] While this may not be sustainable in the long term, it is a great place to be while I am young, single, and do not have any dependents. Many of you will be in a similar situation upon graduation and should take advantage of this unique period in your life.

In the future, I expect the workforce to become much more distributed as companies become increasingly flexible in embracing remote work. However, it is usually the case that you must start working in person at the headquarters to build rapport before a company will trust you to start working remotely.

As someone who grew up in the Midwest, I can acknowledge how difficult it is to uproot your life and pursue a role in a megacity. However, this change does not have to be permanent. After a few years in a big city, you will have the opportunity to take your experience, knowledge, and capital to either a smaller city or a more rural area and separate yourself from the pack.

Key Theme 2: Technological Advances Will Radically Change the Workforce

At the heart of the rapid changes to the U.S. workforce are innovative technologies. In particular, advances in robotics and artificial intelligence will continue to give rise to increased automation and efficiency. These advances will cause growth in certain roles and industries while causing contractions in others.

For instance, health professionals, STEM professionals, and business/legal professionals could see employment growth of +48%, +37% and 20%, respectively, from 2017-2030. Alternatively, office support, food service, and production works/ machine operations roles are likely to see decreases of -11%, -5% and -5%, respectively, during the same period. Ideally, you should gravitate towards industries and professions that are strengthened or not hurt by automation and technological advances.

My previous statement is easier said than done, especially when experts predict that close to 40% of Americans are in occupational categories that could shrink by 2030 and that 8-9% of jobs by 2030 will be ones that barely exist today.[35,36]

Given the difficulty in trying to decipher which professions will grow the most in the future, the next best step you can take is to place a strong emphasis on continued skill development after college. While it's impossible to list all the skills that will be most important in the future, research suggests that with machines taking over routine and physical tasks, the demand for those with socioemotional, creative, technological, and higher level cognitive skills will rise.[37]

By continuing to develop your skills to match with the evolving needs of the economy, you can position yourself to be a more dynamic professional and succeed no matter which ways new technological advances change the makeup of the job market.

Key Theme 3: Focus on Your Personal Brand

For previous generations, the tried and true path to success was to find a stable role in a company, ride it out for a few decades, and be compensated handsomely for your loyalty. That is why the line between an employee's personal brand and the company brand used to be thin to non-existent.

That is no longer the case today. As of 2018, the average employee tenure was only 4.2 years.[38] This trend has been driven by employees and employers alike. With more transparency around salary and the internet making it easier than ever to discover and apply for new roles, many professionals are choosing to leave early for better opportunities. Companies also have more tools than ever to track down top talent and many have shown a willingness to part with long-tenured employees if it makes sense for the business.

To thrive in today's professional environment, it is vital that you grow your personal brand and influence online. A strong personal brand will open up more doors, which is vital in an age in which fluidity between companies remains high.

I talked with tech influencer and startup founder, Tim Salau, about the importance of personal brand. At the time of our video call, Tim had already amassed hundreds of thousands of followers across different online channels. This following has bought him influence in multiple domains and opened new doors that have allowed him to grow his career. One of the things he said that really stuck out to me was that every professional should be building their personal brand through active social media channels. He stated that employees shouldn't be so busy building their employers' brands that they forget to build and invest in their own brand.

While many professionals may be hesitant to take the leap, Tim pointed out that smart organizations understand that their employees' personal brands collectively create the company's brand. By investing in their employees and encouraging them to build their personal brands in a respectable way, companies are making a positive investment in their future.

The Final Round Interview That Wasn't

Austin, TX, November 2016 (My Last Semester of College)
I looked up as the flight attendant who stopped at our row. "Anything to drink?" she asked with a smile. "I'll take a diet coke with ice please." I turned back to stare out of my window at the blue sky with white clouds below. I felt conflicted as I awaited our descent into Austin. I had made a difficult decision, but I wasn't sure it was the right one.

The week before, I had been invited to Austin for a final round interview with IBM for a position in product management. To be honest, I didn't even know that much about IBM prior to the interview. I just wanted it because it was a PM role in Austin. I had spent the previous two summers working in Austin at Dell. I had made amazing friends, fallen in love with the city, and thought I was even falling for a girl. For these reasons, I wanted the role so badly that I had actually declined my final round interview at Intuit because, as fate would have it, the two final round interviews landed on the same day and rescheduling wasn't an option. When large companies set up final round interviews for some positions, the schedules are usually set because they fly in a batch of candidates all at once. I felt guilty because I had already accepted Intuit's invitation but when the IBM interview came in at the last minute, I needed to make a decision. The night before, I told the Intuit recruiter that I was coming down with an illness so I would not be getting on the plane to Intuit's headquarters in Mountain View the next morning. The truth was that I actually would be getting on a plane, just one that was heading to another destination.

When we finally landed, I was greeted with an unfamiliar feeling of cold air in Texas. I hopped in my Uber and took it to the boutique hotel that IBM had booked for the candidate group. That night, we wined and dined at a four-star restaurant, while current IBM product managers were brought in to impress the prospective new hires. At this point, I knew the drill. I had been interviewing for months and felt that I could convince anyone I was the right person for any job. Towards the end of the night, while some of the other candidates were gathering to grab one last drink, I politely declined and went to my hotel room. I knew that interviews should be all business. The interview the next day was a breeze. I noticed that most of the other candidates lacked technical degrees or had never interviewed for a PM role before. I had made it my primary goal to land a PM job after college, and no one was going to stop me.

I was studying in my apartment the following week when the call came in. "Congratulations, Alex, we'd like to extend you an offer of Associate Product Manager at IBM!" When I hung up the phone a few minutes later, I didn't feel as excited as I thought I would. When the offer letter landed in my inbox that night, it felt generic and my enthusiasm was further dampened. I could feel myself getting restless, so I slipped on a pair of gym shorts and a sweatshirt and jogged through the snow to the campus gym on the south end of campus. As I was resting between sets, I felt my phone's vibration. The text was from Kevin Kirn, the Intuit director I had interviewed with on campus. "Hey Alex, It's Kevin. I know you weren't able to make the final round interview, but I really think you belong here. I've talked to the recruiter and we can set up a remote final round interview. It's yours if you want it." I wiped the sweat from my brow as I processed the message. I didn't know what to think.

A few days later, I found myself readjusting the camera on my laptop. It felt weird to be wearing a collared shirt in my bedroom, but it was the one place I could ensure that the wifi would work and it would be quiet. By the time the remote interview was over, I knew I was getting an offer. Sure enough, the offer email landed in my inbox just a few hours later, and it was a solid one. The offer came with a starting salary of six figures plus additional equity. I suddenly had to make another critical decision.

My dad picked me up for Thanksgiving that weekend. On the ride home, I sat in silence and looked out the window. During Thanksgiving dinner, I hardly touched my plate. I was in a deep state of contemplation and it seemed the more I thought about my options, the less clear my decision became. How could I leave behind all of the relationships I had made in Austin, in pursuit of a job in a city where I knew practically zero people? On the plus side, Silicon Valley represented everything I wanted to do and had been working towards for years. I also began to realize how fortunate I was to be able to have a decision to make. I thought about how many of my friends were struggling to even land interviews, and here I was stressing out over which of two great offers to take.

By the time I made it back to campus, I still hadn't made up my mind. I had made multiple calls to people at both companies and while they had all given me great advice, no one could decide for me. I looked out my apartment window where snow was beginning to fall again on the street below. As I stood there, I began breaking down in my mind what was the true difference between the two offers. The IBM offer represented security and comfort, I knew what Austin was all about, and I knew I could make it down in Texas. Intuit, on the other hand, represented the unknown. Having to meet people all over again would force me out of my comfort zone and while I had had a lot of success working on projects in Madison, I wondered if I could cut it in Silicon Valley.

Suddenly, I got a rush of adrenaline. I couldn't explain where it came from or why it struck me at that moment, but suddenly I knew where I wanted to go. I slowly pulled my phone out of my pocket, scrolled down my contact list and pressed call. "Gabby? Hey it's Alex. I just wanted to let you know that I will be accepting the offer. I can't wait to get started at Intuit."

I hung up the phone and stared back out the window. After years of sleepless nights in the library, red bulls for breakfast, career fairs, interviews, and plane rides around the country, I had finally landed my first job. It was time to enter the real world.

CHAPTER 12:

The Real World

I used to think that college would be the most fun and challenging time period of my entire life, and then I entered the real world. While college is an amazing bubble and a truly unique experience, it doesn't last forever. The good news is that if you play your cards right, you can position yourself to start living an even better life after graduation.

Let's assume for a minute that everything goes according to plan. After many late nights of studying mixed with a healthy dose of clubs, internships, networking events, and socializing, you finally leave college with that expensive piece of paper and a professional opportunity lined up. Now what?

The short answer is that there are a lot of other things you need to start doing and in many ways, the real work has just begun. However, that isn't the purpose of this book. My goal is to give you advice on how to navigate college in the current environment in order to find success. Based on the definition I gave earlier, if you have a degree and a job with a promising future, you will have achieved at least some level of success. This success can be soured though if you don't take a few important first steps upon graduation. I want to end by discussing those steps and then I will feel confident that you all are truly ready to succeed long term.

Shoring Up Your Financial Foundations

It's the modern day college horror story: highly accomplished student graduates with an amazing degree and awesome career path, but begins life after college drowning in debt. Whether or not this depicts your situation, you can quickly find yourself in poor financial standing if you pick up poor financial habits upon graduation. While I was working on Mint at Intuit, I learned just how much most Americans struggle with their personal finances. For instance, did you know that close to 40% of Americans can't even cover a $400 emergency expense?[39]

This struggle was on full display when Intuit sent me to Atlanta to do field research for a new financial feature being launched. As I sat in the kitchens of Atlanta residents and listened to them talk about their finances, I learned that many of them were buried in debt and hanging on by a thread. One of the common themes was that they hadn't been prepared by the education system to handle their finances, including those with college degrees.

While you won't be able to achieve full financial literacy simply by reading this book, I feel I would be doing you a disservice if I didn't at least discuss the fundamentals. Below are the most important aspects of your financial health that you should work out immediately upon graduation.

Student Loan Payments

If you do have student loans, it's important that you take control of them and not the other way around. There are a few ways in which you can take control of your student loans. The first is understanding just how much your student loans are going to cost you. This means understanding the initial loan value you took out and how much extra you will end up paying back over time due to interest rates. Once you have this understanding, you can start to work backwards and find confidence in knowing you can form a plan to get to $0 owed.

You should also do your research ahead of time to make sure that when you take out a loan it is at the best rate possible. While there aren't a lot of choices for student loans, you should explore all available options. At a high-level you have two different options for lenders, federal (government) and private (banks or financial institutions). There are a number of online tools that allow you to do these checks yourself and ensure you are getting the best interest rate.

When you do graduate and land a great job, that is when you can set your sights on knocking out your student loan payments. The key is to try to pay your loans off in the smartest and most realistic way . If possible, this means paying it off faster than required since the longer you take, the longer you will feel the effects of interest. In order to pay off your loans faster, you can take steps such as setting up auto-payments, sticking to a biweekly payment plan or calling your loan servicer to have them apply overpayments to your current balance. If you're having trouble keeping track of your different student loans, you might want to consider a student loan consolidation, although this is usually only available for federal loans.

If you have good financial standing, another step you can take is to try to refinance your student loans. By refinancing your student loans, you can essentially secure a new loan at a new interest rate that should be lower than your initial rate, allowing you to save money overall. There are implications to this such as losing eligibility for Income-Driven Repayment plans, loan forgiveness programs, or capability for postponing payments.

To conclude, while student loans can be a serious burden, this is often the cost of being a part of the modern college system. That is why it is important to make sure you become educated about handling this debt, start off with a solid handle on your student loan repayment plan, and exercise discipline in making payments. You want to remember college as a good experience with a great outcome and not something that drags you down for your entire life.

The Credit Score

Though I worked on one of the most popular personal finance apps in the world for two years, and even wrote many articles about the credit score, I admit that I still don't fully understand all of the intricacies of the credit system. However, I do know enough to offer information about the basics and advice about how to keep your credit score as high as possible.

The credit system is a way for financial institutions to measure the likelihood of an individual to repay a loan. Essentially, your credit score reflects how trustworthy you are as a borrower. The primary tool used in the U.S. to prove an individual's creditworthiness is the credit score. With a solid credit score, you will be able to secure a loan whenever you need it to buy a car, house, or other large purchase in the future. When lending institutions consider you for a loan, the decision about the size of the loan and the interest rate will be largely based on your credit standing.

The six key areas that affect your credit score, in order of importance, are the following:

Credit Score Factors

1. Payment History
2. Credit Card Utilization Rate
3. Derogatory Marks
4. Average Age of Credit Lines
5. Total Amount of Credit Lines Opened
6. Number of Hard Inquiries Against You*

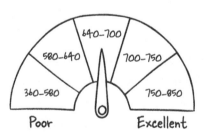

Note a credit score check via an app counts as a soft inquiry. A hard inquiry is only processed when you actually apply for a new credit line.

This isn't a book on personal finance; however, I encourage you to check out my advice online at **TheModern-College.com/creditscore** for an overview of how to master your credit score.

Spending and Saving Habits

In order to have financial success, you need to establish effective spending and saving habits. There is no one method for doing this but I can offer some tips that have worked for me. For starters, automate your finances as much as possible. This includes bill payments, loan payments, and savings contributions. If you start a job with any sort of company-sponsored retirement plan (e.g., 401k) in which the company will match your contribution up to a certain percentage, it almost always makes sense to contribute the maximum amount. Contributing to these accounts early will allow you to take advantage of compound interest and also shield some of your earnings from taxes. If you are someone like me who lacks natural financial discipline, this is the best way to ensure you pay all your bills, have a cushion in savings, and have begun to prepare for a financially secure retirement.

After automating your finances, you will hopefully still have some amount of discretionary income remaining each month. How you choose to spend it is up to you. I don't think it's my place to tell you how to spend your money since we all have different needs and interests. However, I urge you not to spend beyond your means. The moment you begin taking on debt you can't pay off is the moment you will begin to be in financial trouble.

With the ease of using credit cards for expenses, you may find yourself unclear how you're actually spending your money. If so, the best thing you can do is start tracking your spending more closely. As Peter Drucker famously said, "If you can't measure it, you can't improve it." There are many personal finance apps with basic features such as syncing with your financial accounts, providing alerts related to money movements, and displaying historical trends in your spending habits. I worked on the personal finance app called Mint but there are many other personal financial apps and they each take a slightly different angle. I've included some of my favorites at **TheModernCollege.com/finances**.

Broaden Your Horizons

For most of my early life, I spent my days within the borders of Wisconsin. I was fortunate enough to go on a few family vacations to the east coast or out of the country each year but, overall, I had a very narrow view of the world. College did a lot to expand this world view but at the end of the day I was still attending a Wisconsin state college and surrounded by many students who had a very similar world view to myself.

From the moment I walked off the stage at graduation, I knew I wanted to see more of the world. By adopting this mindset, I formed a habit that I continue to this day, which is actively getting out of my comfort zone. It began with a 36-day solo backpacking trip around Europe. During this time, I ate foods I had never tried, met people that didn't speak the same language as me, and saw landmarks that I had once read about in books. At times, it was uncomfortable, such as sleeping in 16-person hostel rooms. At other times it was scary, like getting handcuffed by Paris police for a subway misunderstanding (a story for another time). But more than anything, it was fulfilling.

College teaches you how to think more openly and it's important that you continue to flex this muscle for the rest of your life. You owe it to yourself to continue to expand your world view after college. If you leave college without having this outlook, then you've missed out on a major aspect of the college experience.

Bring Others with You

When you first enter college, you won't even be thinking about the end, at least if you're like me you won't be. During your college experience, time may seem to move slowly and during finals, it will feel as if time has grinded to a halt. But, of course, college eventually comes to an end.

My own college experience ended on a snowy day in December. I looked over my computer networking final exam one last time, walked to the front of the classroom, set it on top of the stack of other exams, shook my professor's hand, and walked towards the exit. When I reached the steps of the lecture hall outside, my friend Nic Harsy (a marine and absolute legend) was already waiting with a cold beer in hand. We shotgunned our beers together and gave each other a congratulatory hug. We had both made it.

Over the coming months, I would embark upon a trip around the world and then migrate across the country to begin my new life in California. This transition involved moving away from the closest people in my life, including my family and childhood friends. I hadn't truly realized how much they meant to me until the day they were no longer a short drive away.

Some of you will find yourself in the same position because you have obtained an opportunity in a place far away from all that has been familiar to you. Others of you may have already made this leap when you went to college. Regardless of where you land, one thing will be true, which is that your connections will fan out significantly after graduation. In previous chapters, I discussed the importance of your network in college, and the time and effort you should dedicate in expanding it while in school. It would be an absolute shame if you let your college network go to waste once you enter the real world. That is why it is important that you bring your network and close connections with you after finishing school. Bringing your network with you means picking up the phone and calling those you care about most on a regular basis. It also means investing the time and resources to visit them and your alma mater whenever possible.

The world is big, but technology has made it much smaller. With some effort and a little patience, you can take one of the most important aspects of college with you no matter where you end up.

The Drive Across America

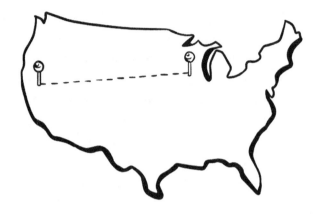

America, March 2017

The wind whipped across my face as I stepped out of the car. My legs felt like lead as I attempted to stretch them out next to the gas pump. "I'm going to run inside, you want anything?" I could barely hear Ivan over the wind. "Yeah, just grab me a juice or something," I shouted back.

I grabbed the cold plastic handle and shoved it into the gas tank. As I stood waiting for the tank to fill, I looked out towards the mountains in the distance. We had just crossed over into Wyoming and while it was fairly desolate, it was beautiful in its own way. The initial emotions of leaving home had subsided over the last day of driving. What was initially a feeling of fear and sadness had been replaced with excitement for the road ahead. "This is what it should feel like," I thought to myself. The feelings of excitement and promise I had were what I had always hoped college would eventually deliver. The promise of a new journey. A new life even. And deliver it did.

When I heard the clink of the gas handle, and I glanced at the digits on the screen, I didn't think anything of it. I had an income now and suddenly what would have been a scary price in college was just a concept that I handled with the little blue plastic card in my wallet.

For the next two days, Ivan and I talked about our plans for the next year, caught up on stories, and listened to a mix of podcasts and the radio. We looked on in awe at the open plains of Wyoming. We stopped for dinner to meet my mom in Salt Lake City, who was in town for a tradeshow. We pulled over to take pictures with Ivan's professional camera on the salt flats on the way out of Utah. I looked on in awe as the terrain turned from snow covered to sand covered as we crossed into Nevada. A small dust storm caught us by surprise at one point and we half laughed, half tensed up as the car rocked while we sped through it. When we finally reached the California border, I blasted "California" by Tupac through my speakers. "California, knows how to party!" I laughed and shouted as we trekked through the mountains and entered the final leg.

As we crawled through traffic over the Bay Bridge, I took out my phone and took a picture of downtown San Francisco. "My new city" I captioned it before posting it to my Snapchat story. Back home in Wisconsin, many of my friends would be following my posts and I didn't want to disappoint.

When we finally turned onto my street that afternoon, there was a slight drizzle coming down. We pulled into the tiny garage below my house. It was so narrow that I had to fold the side windows on my car. Ivan and I each grabbed a bag, and climbed the steps to my new apartment. "So this is what $2,000 a month in rent gets you," I joked as we walked into my apartment for the first time. We plopped the bags down into the last empty bedroom in the apartment. "You want me to help you unpack?" Ivan asked. I shook my head. "Nah man, you've only got one night here before you fly back. Let's go out and have some fun."

Before I turned to leave my room, I noticed my framed glass diploma sticking out from underneath one of my garbage bags filled with clothes. I bent down and picked it up, holding it in my hands for a moment. "You going to hang that up on your wall?" Ivan asked. I looked over at him and then back at the diploma. This little piece of paper was supposed to embody four and a half years of my life. Every exam I had taken, textbook I had read, beer I had drank, all for this tiny slip of paper. I shook my head and laughed. "Nah man, this paper doesn't actually mean anything." I tossed it onto the stack of clothes in my closet, turned off the lights and walked out of my room.

ACKNOWLEDGMENTS

I poured my mind, heart, and soul into Modern College, but the reality is that this book wouldn't have happened without the amazing support network I have in my life. First and foremost, I'd like to thank my family.

Eileen and Mark, the greatest privilege I've ever been given in this life is having you two as my parents. Mom, I will never lose sight of the fact that you made it your life's purpose to raise your two sons. Your involvement in the local community, our school board, and my education was crucial to my development. You taught an unremarkable young boy with attention issues that if he gave his all in every facet of life and constantly sought to learn, he could be anything he wanted.

Dad, I don't know how you did it but you somehow managed to be there for all the important moments, even while spending 100+ days every year on the road supporting the family. I attribute whatever mental toughness and competitiveness I have to the collegiate wrestler that is my father. Thank you for teaching me what it means to be a man and how to lift others up along the way.

Austin, thank you for being my best friend and also a key inspiration for this book. I still remember the day you were born and how proud I was to become a big brother. Without you, it would have been easy for me to leave college in the rearview for good once I walked across the stage for graduation. Watching you face your own struggles and find your personal path to success in college forced me to think critically about how to make sure my advice was relevant to all students. I'll always be there as a mentor for you and hope that by allowing me to test this advice on you first, it made the journey a little bit less bumpy.

I am also fortunate to have the strongest extended family a person could ever ask for. My grammy Barbara Valaitis and grandpa Glenn Hendry in particular have always been strong champions for my educational journey, including helping finance my high school and college educations. To the rest of the Valaitis and Hendry sides of my family, your support has been crucial on this journey. There were a lot of times I wanted to give up or didn't think I was capable of writing this book. You were all there to support me in our in-person conversations and online whenever I made a post. We are a big family of learners and without that culture embedded into my life from all of you, this would not have been a venture I would have ever considered pursuing.

To my friends, I'd first like to start by thanking you all for being patient with me. This book has been such a focus of mine for the past year and a half that I didn't reach out to some of you as much as I should have, and for the ones I did reach out to, thank you for listening to me ramble on about this book. I'm proud to say that I have great friends all over the world, and I am grateful for the diverse perspectives you have given me on college and life. There's too many of you to mention by name, but a special shout out to my Wisconsin,

San Francisco, Austin, and East Coast friend groups, you all know who you are.

My LinkedIn crew has also been a critical part of this journey. Without a doubt, my passion for this book has been fueled by working with ridiculously smart people that care a lot about the areas I wrote about in Modern College. I'd like to thank the Pages, Elevate, LMS, and Product teams for encouraging me to pursue this book. Specifically, I'd like to thank my manager, Rishi Jobanputra, for never questioning my ability to lead important projects at work while also balancing this book.

A very special shout out goes to my close friend and co-worker, Julia Abelsky. You've made too big of an impact on me and this book over the past year to squeeze you in with anyone else. From being my part-time book consultant to nursing me back to health after my severe arm injury, I can say that I figuratively and literally would not have made it here without you. Thank you for constantly pushing me to up my game and for always answering my late night Facetimes whenever I needed advice.

To all the teachers and advisors I've had in my life, I want to thank you all for helping me to stay engaged and to never stop seeking knowledge. Between Hales Corners Elementary, Whitnall Middle School, Marquette University High School, and UW-Madison I've been blessed with a world-class education at every turn. You all are real-life heroes.

For those of you who let me share pieces of your advice or life in this book, I can't thank you enough. I am just one person who has walked one path. By lending your insights to this book, you will allow far more people to connect to Modern

College than would have been possible if I had to tell everything from my own perspective. Special thanks to everyone who let me name drop them in the book or shared insights for different sections.

Lastly, I'd like to thank the team who worked on Modern College. When I completed the first draft of Modern College, I had an average piece at best. With your collective help, we transformed it into a great piece that will redefine the way that parents and students look at the higher education system. Barbara Schirmer and Jennifer Rees, thank you for your diligent work on the edits while allowing me to keep my voice. David Provolo, you're a creative genius and I appreciate your patience, which helped lead to an incredible cover and interior production. Amanda Valaitis, you're more talented than you'll ever realize and your illustrations helped bring this book to life. And to all of the people who will play a key part in marketing this book and spreading the word about Modern College, I thank you all in advance. I can't wait to bring this work to the masses!

LAUNCH TEAM MEMBERS

Aaron Nichols
Armando Juan Carlos Saafir
Arnav Kaul
Ashar Malik
Austin Valaitis
Christina Ghinos
Christopher Call
Dhrumil Patel
Dillon Stuart
Ed Hendry
Garrett Allen
Greg Hendry
Gregory M Jones
Ivan Herrada
James Kim
Jameson Zaballos
Julia Abelsky
Kasey Altman
Keira Valaitis
Kevin Cj Bannerman
Kris Dimo
Logan Dirkx
Matthew Starr
Michael Beiermeister

Michael Bonin
Mike Fix
Mitchell Kim
Nancy Wilkes
Nathan Dupont
Nick Clarizio
Ryan McClure
Sammi Sison
Santiago Chavez
Silpa Reddy
Sydney Russakov
Tai Bendit
Ted Schelble
Tess Hendry
Trevor Thompson
Tyler Fischer
Vangelis Dimopoulos
Willy Gonzalez
Xiao He
Yazeed Sabri
Zack Braun
Zane Homsi

AFTERWORD:
The College of the Future

Milwaukee, Wisconsin, May 2020

When I originally typed out the conclusion to this book in January of 2020, I did it from a coffee shop in San Francisco. Over the next few months, as I was putting the finishing touches on the manuscript, a global catastrophe began unfolding that few saw coming. COVID-19, aka the coronavirus, has caught the world completely flat-footed and will likely go down as one of, if not the defining event, of my generation. Unlike 9/11 or the great recession, which I was too young to fully process, I understand the magnitude of this event on a visceral level. Like most people, I'm experiencing a mixed bag of emotions ranging from fear to sadness. It will take me a long time to fully process what is happening, but one thing I know for sure is that the world will look fundamentally different when we come out of it.

Certain areas of life will be exponentially more impacted than others, and higher education falls on the most affected end of the spectrum. This fallout was on full display when I went to visit my younger brother, Austin, over the past weekend. Austin elected to continue living in his house in Madison, despite the fact that the campus has been shut down indefinitely. This decision was largely driven by the fact that most of my brother's friends are in their last semester (Austin is doing one extra semester).

During the visit, I sat (at the recommended six feet of distance) and listened to my brother's friends who were graduating in just a few short weeks. I listened to them complain about the lack of quality in their online courses this semester and about how sad they were that their commencement would be completely online. They were being robbed of the life highlight of walking across the stage for graduation and had missed the opportunity to say proper goodbyes to the close connections they had made over the past four years. This sadness quickly turned to fear when I asked them how they felt about the next chapter. Some of them told me how they had been expecting to graduate into one of the hottest job markets in history but were, instead, having their internships and full-time offers rescinded. They asked me for advice on how to adjust to this changing landscape and while I gave them some basic advice, I also admitted that I needed more time to reflect before I could give them a better answer.

As I sit here in my dad's office re-writing the final lines of this book, I now know the answer I will give to my brother and his friends the next time they ask for my advice. I will tell them to read Modern College.

Initially, when I began reflecting on the impact of COVID-19 on higher education, I was fearful that the fallout from the pandemic would render all of the content I had created over the past year and a half no longer relevant. In reality, the effect will be just the opposite. The coronavirus didn't change the course of higher education, it simply accelerated us down the path we were already on. Or put another way, the coronavirus is about to make the Modern College materialize faster than even I was expecting.

When I started writing this book, I fancied myself a fortune teller; now I just sound like a reporter. Some of the boldest predictions and forward-thinking advice I laid out when I first started writing on this subject over a year ago will now seem obvious. But the good news is that everything I have stated in this book is more relevant than ever before.

After COVID-19, the true purposes of college will be exposed and many universities will not survive as a result. The top colleges will thrive as their value proposition of prestige will resonate as strongly as ever given their name recognition and their large endowments will allow them to ride out any short term demand softness from having to go remote for a few semesters. Public universities will survive, as their lower relative prices will make them more attractive to those who might previously have attended middle-tier private colleges. These middle-tier private colleges will be hit the hardest. Many of them, which were already facing financial hardships, will be forced to close for good if they can't open up their campuses in the fall. Remote classes have pulled back the curtains on the type of education students are really getting in lecture halls, and many parents don't like what they are seeing. Trying to convince parents or students to pay $40,000 for a few hours of mediocre Zoom classes every week isn't going to end well for a lot of universities.

For many rising college freshmen and high school seniors, the concept of choosing an alternative path to a 4-year degree will seem much more logical. I predict we will see a drop in 4-year college applications over the next decade, which is something that hasn't happened in over two centuries. In contrast, we will see a rise in many of the other paths such as coding boot camps, trade specializations, and technical schools. This demand for alternative paths should lead to a rapid rise in innovation in the higher ed, online learning, and professional development spaces as talented people begin to realize that a $10 trillion industry is in the process of being disrupted and they will attempt to grab a piece of the pie.[40]

The importance of technical literacy and professional networking will be amplified as recruiting and work become more distributed and virtual. Furthermore, many of the themes I have harped upon in this book, such as building an online presence and focusing on tangible skills, will become critical. Companies will begin to realize that they can source quality candidates outside of the walls of universities, which will force them to place less emphasis on the piece of paper colleges provide as a result.

The Modern College is here to stay and its key themes will only be amplified as we move into the future. In some ways, this will be a good thing, as the shift to online will open up access to more people at a lower cost and prevent many families and young adults from burying themselves in debt for the wrong reasons. On the flip side, many young adults will have a huge void in their lives as the beautifully complex experience of living on campus in pursuit of a 4-year college degree will not be a part of their development. How we fill that void is an important discussion that will define what our country looks like in the decades to come.

— Alex Valaitis

WORKS CITED

National Center for Education Statistics. (2019). The Condition of Education: Undergraduate Retention and Graduation Rates. Institute of Education Sciences, U.S. Department of Education. https://nces.ed.gov/programs/coe/indicator_ctr.asp

Miller, A. (2013, April 30). Milken Institute 2013 Global Conference. https://www.youtube.com/watch?v=vw_Ey9Oip9g

Bennett, W. (2013, April 30). Milken Institute 2013 Global Conference. https://www.youtube.com/watch?v=vw_Ey9Oip9g

Kurt, D. (2019). Student Loan Debt: 2019 Statistics and Outlook. Investopedia. https://www.investopedia.com/student-loan-debt-2019-statistics-and-outlook-4772007

Ryan, C. L., & Bauman, K. (2016). Educational Attainment in the United States: 2015. https://www.census.gov/content/dam/Census/library/publications/2016/demo/p20-578.pdf

College Board. (2019). Trends in College Pricing 2019. https://research.collegeboard.org/pdf/trends-college-pricing-2019-full-report.pdf

The Harris Poll. (2019). Boomerang Generation, Returning to the Nest. TD Ameritrade. https://s2.q4cdn.com/437609071/files/doc_news/research/2019/Boomerang-Generation-Returning-to-the-Nest.pdf

Gladwell, M. (2008). Outliers: The Story of Success. Little, Brown and Company.

College Board. (2019). Trends in College Pricing 2019. https://research.collegeboard.org/pdf/trends-college-pricing-2019-full-report.pdf

Kurt, D. (2019). Student Loan Debt: 2019 Statistics and Outlook. Investopedia. https://www.investopedia.com/student-loan-debt-2019-statistics-and-outlook-4772007

Tatham, M. (2019). Student Loan Debt Climbs to $1.4 Trillion in 2019. Experian. https://www.experian.com/blogs/ask-experian/state-of-student-loan-debt/#s1

Make Lemonade Staff. (2019). Student Loan Debt Statistics for 2020. Make Lemonade. https://www.makelemonade.co/student-loan-debt-statistics/

World Bank Group. (2017). Life Expectancy at Birth, Total (Years)-United States. The World Bank.

Wallace, N. (2016). The Best Jobs for People Who Want to be Self-Employed. SmartAsset. https://smartasset.com/career/best-self-employed-jobs

Mike Rowe Works Foundation. (2020). https://www.mikeroweworks.org/

Indeed. (2020). Skilled Trades Salaries in the United States. https://www.indeed.com/cmp/Skilled-Trades/salaries

Course Report. (2018). The Growth of Coding Bootcamps 2018. https://www.coursereport.com/reports/2018-coding-bootcamp-market-size-research

Lambda School. (2020). What is an ISA? https://lambdaschool.com/isa

Community College Review. (2020). Average Community College Tuition Cost. https://www.communitycollegereview.com/avg-tuition-stats/national-data

Year Out Group. (2018). Gap Year Statistics to Help Take the Leap. https://yearoutgroup.org/gap-year-statistics/

Ravikant, N. (2019). How to Get Rich: Every Episode. https://nav.al/rich

Kahneman, D. (2013). Thinking, Fast and Slow. Farrar, Straus, and Giroux.

Galloway, S. (2020). Post-Corona, Higher Ed. No Mercy/No Malice. https://www.profgalloway.com/post-corona-higher-ed

Burning Glass Technologies. (2013). The Art of Employment: How Liberal Arts Graduates Their Labor Market Prospects. https://www.burning-glass.com/wp-content/uploads/BG-TReportLiberalArts.pdf

Fleming, N., & Bonwell, C. (2019). How Do I Learn Best: A Student's Guide to Improved Learning. https://vark-learn.com/wp-content/uploads/2019/07/How-Do-I-Learn-Best-Sample.pdf

Graham, P. (2014). Before the Startup. http://www.paulgraham.com/before.html

Granovetter, M. S. (1973). The Strength of Weak Ties. American Journal of Sociology, 73(6), 1360-1380. https://sociology.stanford.edu/sites/g/files/sbiybj9501/f/publications/the_strength_of_weak_ties_and_exch_w-gans.pdf

Brown, M., Setren, E., & Topa, G. (2014). Do Informal Referrals Lead to Better Matches? Evidence from a Firm's Employee Referral System (IZA Discussion Paper No. 8175). SSRN. https://ssrn. com/abstract=2441471

Garlinghouse, M. (2019). Closing the Network Gap. https://blog. linkedin.com/2019/september/26/closing-the-network-gap

LinkedIn. (n.d.). About LinkedIn. https://about.linkedin.com/

Jobvite. (2019). 2019 Recruiting Benchmark Report: Fuel Optimization Efforts with Exclusive Industry Data. https://www. jobvite.com/wp-content/uploads/2019/10/2019-Jobvite-Recruiting-Benchmark-Report.pdf

Lund, S., Manyika, J., Segel, L. H., Dua, A., Hancock, B., Rutherford, S., & Macon, B. (2019). The Future of Work in America: People and Places, Today and Tomorrow. McKinsey Global Institute. https://www.mckinsey.com/~/media/McKinsey/ Featured%20Insights/Future%20of%20Organizations/The%20 future%20of%20work%20in%20America%20People%20and%20 places%20today%20and%20tomorrow/MGI-The-Future-of-Work-in-America-Report-July-2019.ashx

Galloway, S. (2017). Unsolicited Career Advice. https://www. youtube.com/watch?v=1T22QxTkPoM

Rent Jungle. (2020). Rent trend data in San Francisco, California. https://www.rentjungle.com/average-rent-in-san-francisco-rent-trends/

Manyika, J., Lund, S., Chui, M., Bughin, J., Woetzel, J., Batra , P., Ko, R., & Sanghvi, S. (2017). Jobs Lost, Jobs Gained: Workforce Transitions in a Time of Automation. McKinsey Global Institute. https://www.mckinsey.com/~/media/mckinsey/featured%20

insights/Future%20of%20Organizations/What%20the%20
future%20of%20work%20will%20mean%20for%20jobs%20
skills%20and%20wages/MGI-Jobs-Lost-Jobs-Gained-Report-De-
cember-6-2017.ashx

Lin, J. (2011). Technological Adaptation, Cities, and New Work.
Review of Economics and Statistics, 93(2), 554-574. Earlier
version working paper available at https://papers.ssrn.com/sol3/
papers.cfm?abstract_id=1456545

Bughin, J., Hazan, E., Lund, S., Dahlström, P., Wiesinger, A., &
Subramaniam, A. (2018). Skill Shift: Automation and the Future
of the Workforce. McKinsey Global Institute. https://www.mck-
insey.com/featured-insights/future-of-work/skill-shift-automa-
tion-and-the-future-of-the-workforce

U.S. Bureau of Labor Statistics. (2018). Economic News Release:
Employee Tenure Summary. https://www.bls.gov/news.release/
tenure.nr0.htm

Bahney, A. (2018). 40% of Americans Can't Cover a $400 Emer-
gency Expense. CNN. https://money.cnn.com/2018/05/22/pf/
emergency-expenses-household-finances/index.html

HolonIQ. (2018). Education in 2030: Five Scenarios for the Future of Learning and Talent. https://www.holoniq.com/wp-con-
tent/uploads/2020/01/HolonIQ-Education-in-2030.pdf

About the Author

Alex Valaitis is a product manager who has worked for multiple top tech companies including LinkedIn, Intuit, and Dell. He is a graduate of the University of Wisconsin-Madison where he received bachelor's degrees in Computer Science and Economics. In his free time, Alex enjoys blogging, following F1 racing, and hunting for the tastiest burrito in San Francisco.

Made in the USA
Coppell, TX
25 June 2020

29249454R00135